The Road to Rannoch and The Summer Isles

THE ROAD TO RANNOCH

AND

THE SUMMER ISLES

ISLE ORONSAY AND MAINLAND PEAKS ROUND LOCH HOURN

Frontispiece

THE ROAD TO RANNOCH

AND

THE SUMMER ISLES

T. RATCLIFFE BARNETT

WITH 22 *ILLUSTRATIONS*
BY ROBERT M. ADAM
AND 2 DRAWINGS

JOHN GRANT BOOKSELLERS LTD.
EDINBURGH: 31 GEORGE IV. BRIDGE
LONDON: 98 GREAT RUSSELL STREET, W.C.

1944

FIRST EDITION   .   .   *July* 1924
REPRINTED   .   .   *November* 1924
     ,,   .   .   .   *May* 1926
     ,,   .   .   .   *June* 1930
NEW AND REVISED EDITION   .   1944

PRINTED IN GREAT BRITAIN BY
OLIVER AND BOYD LTD., EDINBURGH

TO

KENNETH MACLEOD

BARD OF THE ISLES : GLEANER OF GAELIC LEGENDARY : AND
HIGH PRIEST OF THE GREAT MYSTERIES—IN MEMORY OF
A DAY IN MULL WHEN HE MADE US SEE, WITH COLUMBA'S
EYES, THE VISIONS ROUND THE WHITE TABLE—THESE PAPERS
ARE DEDICATED BY A WAYFARING MAN WHO HAS SEEN SOME-
THING OF GOD'S BEAUTY IN THE BENS, THE GLENS, AND THE
ISLANDS, AND HAS FOUND MANY A FORTUNE IN THE HEART
OF HIS FELLOW-TRAVELLERS

FOREWORD

MOST of these papers, the record of many happy days, have appeared in *The Scotsman*. One was published in *The Glasgow Herald*. Three are printed here for the first time.

I am most grateful to the following, who no longer travel with us : Mr E. V. Lucas, for granting me permission to quote from a poem which first appeared in *A Little of Everything*; Mr Lloyd Osbourne, for leave to make use of odd verses from the Songs of Robert Louis Stevenson; Mr Geoffrey Winthrop Young, for two poems quoted from his *Wind and Hill*. Also to Messrs Longmans, Green & Co. for the verse quoted from Andrew Lang's " Song of the Bow "; and to the Rev. Kenneth Macleod, the minister of the Isle of Gigha, for one or two of his translations of Gaelic Legendary. Nor must I forget to salute those who dearly loved Scotland, but who no longer walk with us on the old roads.

" A soft path for the far traveller ! "

T. R. B.

March 1944

CONTENTS

ix

ILLUSTRATIONS

xi

BUNDLE AND GO

O weary are the feet that tramp the stony streets of June,
And hungry is the gangrel's heart that hears the nameless
     tune ;
For earth's call is a strong call, and it's happiness to
     yield,
And my foot is on the long road that leads me far afield.

  The back was made for bundles and the oxter for the
      pipes,
  So, steep the withie, draw the door, and turn the rusty
      key ;
  For summer's here, and everywhere there's music in the
      air,
  The whaups are on the heather and the white birds on
      the sea !

The road that leads to Rannoch is the gangrel's royal
     way,
But Ben Doran is to climb, with Stob Gour and Inver-
     veigh ;
It taigles us round Tulla, where the red-deer have their
     home,
And the salmon flash like silver where the broken waters
     foam.

O Orchy's stream is my stream, for it keeps me by its side
On the road among the heather where the fairy folks bide ;
In a bed of scented myrtle I lie and hear them sing,
And heather bells are ringing in my dwam of dovering.

Tickled trout are tasty trout, and a weary man must eat ;
So I light my fire at Ba Bridge, and frizzled fish are
*   sweet.*
I give a cry to Kingshouse, Buchaille Etive, and Glencoe,
But the sea-wrack of Leven lures me on, and I must go.

I make a bed of sound sleep in the wood of Lettervore,
And dream of all that happened there in days that are no
*   more ;*
I see the unknown shooter, and the Red Fox is his game ;
But even in dreams I durst not tell the secret of that name.

But there's music in the world yet so long as birds can sing,
And the primrose glades of Appin are wonderful in spring ;
The west wind is my home wind and the tartan's on my
*   knee,*
And a boat rides at anchor on the laughing waves for me.

So I leave the Highland highway, and I hoist the brown
*   sail*
For summer isles of Tir-nan-og, from Barra to Kintail ;
And there upon the snow-white sands and machars of the
*   West*
I seek and find the lost things—the things that I love best.

The back was made for bundles and the oxter for the
pipes,
So, steep the withie, draw the door, and turn the rusty
key ;
For summer's here, and everywhere there's music in the
air,
The whaups are on the heather and the white birds on
the sea !

THE SUMMER ISLES

WHITE WINGS ON SAPPHIRE SEAS

THERE had been no break in the glorious June weather
for weeks. Cloudless skies, soft breezes, and dancing
seas—it was always the same. It was indeed the queen
of summers, to which we shall look back with many
a rare remembrance of magic days and nights spent
among the islands of the West. For me the Sound of
Mull is the outgait of dreams. The sunny sea-lochs of
Clyde are full of their own witchery; but when we
speak of the outside waters we mean the world that lies
on the other side of Kintyre, beyond Crinan, or far up
by Skye and the Hebrides, where the real seas tumble
in from the limitless Atlantic. There you must seek
Tir-nan-og, the Land of Eternal Youth.

We were lying in the bay of Mary's Well. The
morning sun was beating down on the white decks.
The blue reek rose from the cottages on the shore,
where many a goodwife was stirring the early spurtle.
The great sails were hoisted, and flapped pleasantly on
the faint winds. The click-click of the old-fashioned
windlass sounded across the bay, and the anchor trailed
reluctant over the sea floor, where the long-lost treasure
of the Spanish galleon still lies deep down. When at
last the anchor was home, the white sails filled, the
schooner lay over, and we began to slip away from the

anchorage. Slowly the wooded shores were left behind, and we crept past the white lighthouse of Rhu-na-gall, the point of the stranger ; and Bloody Bay, where the Macleans slaughtered Alastair Crotach long ago. Loch Sunart was soon astern, and when we got out by Ardnamurchan, the headland of the sea-nymphs or the great waves, there was nothing before us but the wide Atlantic, with the distant islands lying in its lap. Yonder is Skye, and the Coolins rising like a dim cloud from the sea. Nearer at hand is Rhum of the Ridges, with the sharp peaks of Haskeval and Haleval piercing the sky, and nearer still the Scuir of Eigg rising above the waves.

Skye and Eigg—how the sight of them rouses memories of old clan feuds between those fell fighters, the Macleods and the Macdonalds ! For, one Sunday a company of the Macdonalds sailed for Skye, and found the Macleods of Vaternish in Trumpan Church at prayer. They fastened the door, set fire to the church, and burned every one in it, except one woman, who squeezed herself through a window, and so escaped to raise the countryside with her cries. The Macleods came down on their enemies before they could get away, for it was ebb-tide, and their boats, which had been tied to the arching rocks, hung in the air. The Macleods fought till their last Macdonald enemy was killed, the women of Skye picking up the blunted arrows, sharpening them on the stones, and giving them to their brave men. Then they took the bodies of the Macdonalds, laid them out in a row beneath the turf dyke that had been built to keep out the sea, tumbled the dyke on them, and so buried them. The place is known to this day as the field of the Battle of the Spoiled Dykes. But revenge always followed—

Lewis Township : Valtos on the Shores of Loch Roag

terrific. For, on a sunny winter day the Macleod galleys sailed for Eigg. Not a single Macdonald, man, woman, or child, could be found on the island. So the galleys sailed for Skye again, and while they were at sea a sudden snowstorm swept over the islands, so that when the sun came out again Eigg stood out of the wintry seas like a pearly berg. Then a little black speck appeared on the top of the snow-white isle. It disappeared again. The galleys turned. It was a man doing sentry-go on the Scuir of Eigg. The Macleods returned, traced the man by his footprints in the snow to a great cave below the Scuir, gathered brushwood, set it ablaze at the entrance, and suffocated every Macdonald who was within. Bones under Trumpan Dyke and bones in the cave on Eigg have been found within living memory. A grim tale. But it could be matched with others, as bloody and as cruel, about many a desolate spot on these isles where the sea wind soughs a coronach to-day.

Look around now on this dream of summer beauty, and forget the old clan feuds if you can. The little clouds float like tufts of fairy fleece up in the brilliant blue, and the breeze comes sighing out of the west, rippling the waters until the whole sea is like one vast flashing plain of sapphire. In the noontide heat we creep forward and lie down in the shadow of the foresail. Looking over the gunwale and away down at the cut-water, we see a perfect poem of cool colours, the most delicate greens and blues, being turned up as the stem of the yacht cleaves its way like a knife through the summer sea.

Then, when the wind has fallen, and the water is as calm as glass, we stand stripped in the sun, with hands upraised as for a great adventure, and take a

clean header into the fathomless Atlantic, coming up
again buoyant as a cork. What glory of strength and
thrill of life ! The rush of many waters in the ears,
the cold green deeps on which the eyes have looked
below, the hot white decks again beneath the dripping
limbs !

> " On throat and hair, the quivering ice-stars breaking
>   Like foam of silver wine ;
> Waves of exultant thought in sense awaking
>   Glamour of youth divine.
>
> " Toil to delight, pain to remembered pleasure,
>   Embers to ruddy gold
> Change at thy touch, O life's most usual treasure,
>   Water divinely cold."
>   —GEOFFREY WINTHROP YOUNG.

But soon the wind comes up again, and the white
sails draw. The dulcet tones of a guitar and the sound
of a song float up through an open skylight and mingle
with the sound of plashing seas and creaking spars.
Cailleach Point and Calgary Bay, Coll, Tiree, and the
Treshnish Isles—right out to the Dutchman's Cap we
sail through the golden afternoon—white birds above
us, white clouds in the blue, white shadows on the
shimmering sea—a perfect idyll of pearly summer and
the *Tir-nan-og* of the West.

Or is it the ghostly Coolins ? We creep into Loch
Scavaig on a falling breeze at twilight, and make fast
to the rings on the rocks at the very head of this bottle-
mouthed sea-loch. The great rock masses almost
tumble down on the tiny ship lying still and motionless
in the glassy gloom. The mad stream falls into the sea
with a weird whisper. Coruisk and its abysmal shadows
is just a step over the rocks, and at night the Northern

COOLIN RANGE AND LOCH SCAVAIG

Lights play far up in the lambent sky above the inky glooms of Garsven, as we fall asleep in this wild, unearthly, lost world of sea and rock and sky.

What a glorious coast-line has Skye—in and out of the many sea-lochs—more varied than any other great island of the West—Eishort and Slapin, Scavaig and Brittle, Eynort and Bracadale, Dunvegan and Snizort. The name of Macleod dominates the west of Skye. Macleod's Maidens—three isolated pillars of rock rising out of the sea—stand eternal. Macleod's Tables—great flat remnants of the basalt plain which once covered the island—in the centre of Duirinish. At the head of Dunvegan Loch stands the famous Castle of Macleod—the oldest inhabited castle in Scotland, with one of the longest unbroken lines of ancestry in our land still in it. Tradition has it that the keep has been occupied since the tenth century; but it is, at least, certain that the descendants of Leod have lived there since the day in the thirteenth century when he married the daughter of Macraild Armuinn the Dane. All honour to the last of these veteran chiefs. We shall not soon forget his courtesy when he showed us the Bottle Dungeon which opens weirdly off the drawing-room, Rory More's drinking horn, the Fairy Flag, and all the rest.

Rhum, with its high hills, is well named the Isle of Ridges. Many have sought shelter from the storm in little Loch Scresort. My memories are of the days when Rhum was a desolation, and Old Hookie the Yorkshire keeper bred fighting cocks at Kinloch to supply the miners of his native county in England. An old tame stag, in those days, wandered about the green in front of the plain white house. I suppose electricity and the telegraph have changed Rhum.

But on a summer Sunday morning I have watched men row away in a heavy boat to Isle Oronsay, off the east coast of Skye, a distance of twenty miles and more, for a doctor—and a second boat leave in the afternoon to countermand the first, owing to the recovery of the patient—and the doctor was met and turned somewhere in the Sound of Sleat. A journey by boat of forty miles on the chance of saving a life !

How often are these islands cut off by storm from all communication with the outer world !

> " The white waves foaming to the distant sky."

From this same Loch Scresort we set out on an ugly morning of wind and rain. But the squalls increased, the seas rose, sail was shortened to the utmost limit, and all day we beat and thrashed against the gale till the darkening, only to be driven back to the shelter which we had left. Who that has pounded along in pitch darkness on the great seas between Eigg and Rhum, or out on the Minch between Skye and the Outer Isles, can ever forget the savage power of wind and wave and the sheets of rain ! It was just out here that Stevenson must have faced the force of sea and wind, else he could never have written these words in his immortal Song of Youth :—

> " Mull was astern, Rum on the port.
>   Eigg on the starboard bow :
>   Glory of youth glowed in his soul :
>   Where is that glory now ?
>
>   .   .   .   .   .
>
> " Billow and breeze, islands and seas,
>   Mountains of rain and sun,
>   All that was good, all that was fair,
>   All that was me is gone ! "

Island of Rum

But none who have sought these summer isles or gone in quest of *Tir-nan-og* will ever be content until he has reached the farthest limit of rock and skerry. To set out through the Sound of Harris on the sixty-mile voyage to far St Kilda and back again on the long, low Atlantic swell; to coast up and down and in and out the little lochs of the Long Island from Stornoway to Barra Head; now sailing on laughing seas, with infinite horizons on every side, and the white sands of many a lonely bay gleaming in the sunlight; now shipping great seas in the dark as we swing into Boisdale or Barra, with the green and red sidelights flashing on the yeasty waves—this is to know the seaway to the isles that each must find for himself.

The children of tempest long to return from many a weary wandering on the rim of the world to their little thatch huts on these desolate isles. They cannot forget. So I have seen an elderly woman standing on the fo'c'sle head with a misty gleam in her eyes as the boat drew into Tarbet, Harris. Yonder on the lochside is someone waving from a cottage door. Here on the quayhead an old man greets the mother of his six grandsons, each one of whom now owns his farm in Canada, for it is thirty-five years since the mother left home. I have seen the flaxen-haired, blue-eyed daughters of Viking ancestors, and little black Celts with the colour of the grey seas in their eyes, coming and going between the cities of the South and these wave-washed shores, proud to return to the poor shielings with great tales of the wonder-world they have discovered far from home. I have seen them bringing back their dead across the stormy Minch to Barra Bay and in past Castle Kishmul in the sunset. A cart full of clean-smelling meadow hay and a group of grave-faced friends are waiting. Then a solemn rumbling of wheels as the little company follow their dead over the old road to the west side. There, in the darkening by the white sands, a sound of keening comes from a cottage door.

> " Many a poor black cottage is there ;
>   Grimy with peat smoke,
>   Sending up in the soft evening air
>   Purest of incense,
>   While the low music of Psalm and prayer
>   Rises to heaven.
>   Reared in these dwellings have brave ones been ;
>   Brave ones are still there ;
>   Forth from their darkness on Sunday I've seen
>   Coming pure linen,
>   And, like the linen, the souls were clean
>   Of them that wore it."
>
> —SHERIFF NICOLSON.

There are still men of the mystic soul who search out here, at the back of the world, for the Isle of Lost Youth. Standing on the summit rocks of Gillavel Glas and Skean Tosal, in Harris, with the solemn beauty of the isles lying all about me, I have gazed to the west, past the whaling station and far beyond Soay and Taransay, to that little inland loch on the Atlantic seaboard where the island of Mary Rose lies sleeping in sunshine. There, beyond all reach of the racketing world and on the very edge of mystery, some have gazed right into the sunset and have guessed the meaning of the look which every islesman wears on his face to the end of the hundred thousand days.

II

THE ISLAND OF LEWIS

THE STORY OF THE FIFE SETTLERS

THE roots of many a modern trouble can be traced far back into history, and few people to-day know the fascinating story of the first attempts in the early seventeenth century to colonise the island of Lewis by a band of adventurous Fife gentlemen. Let me tell this almost unbelievable tale as briefly as possible.

The whole range of the Outer Hebrides, from the Butt of Lewis to Barra Head, is often called the Long Island, because, as you thrash your way across the Minch, the whole hundred and twenty miles of islands seem like one long mainland without a break. The largest island by far is the northmost, called Lewis-and-Harris, and the story has to do with Lewis alone.

At the end of the sixteenth century Lewis was possessed by the Siol Torquil, or race of Torquil, while Harris belonged to the Siol Tormod, or race of Tormod, both of these being branches of the fell clan of Macleod. It is indeed from this family that Lewis, or The Lews, as it is often called, takes its name, which means the Land of Leod. The genealogies of the Macleods at this time would make a puzzle chapter in family history. Had not that redoubtable old man of over ninety, Ruari Macleod, the last chief of Lewis, who died in 1595, three wives, a whole quiverful of legitimate sons,

and five natural sons ? Their careers make one of the
greatest family hurly-burlies of war, quarrelling, blood-
shed, murder, and thievery ever written by the pen of
man. But we must reluctantly give all that the go-by
here.

King James VI., just before he went south to
London to take over another throne (thus setting a
precedent for a trip to London which many a canny
Scot has followed since), thought it high time to civilise
his Hebridean subjects by bringing them under the
law, with a view to ending their interminable quarrels
of disputed succession. And he determined to begin
with the Lewis Macleods. For, since the beginning of
time, the island of Lewis seems to have had the reputa-
tion of being a kind of Eldorado which was worth
exploiting.

Did not Dean Munro of the Isles, after a trip there
about 1544, declare that it was " ane fertile, fruitful
country, for the most part all biere " ? Did not
Martin, who wrote his *Description of the Western Isles*
before 1700, actually maintain that gold dust was
found in Harris and North Uist, and that " the teeth
of the sheep which feed there are dyed yellow " with
it ? Did not the late Sir James Matheson, of good
repute, sink hundreds of thousands of pounds in Lewis,
believing that he would get back his money from peat
industries ? And in our own day Lord Leverhulme
made a gigantic try at turning Lewis into a paying
commercial speculation. Little wonder that we were
on the tip-toe of curiosity to see if this island of Lewis
was at last to become a land flowing with milk and
honey, or to remain what it has always seemed to be,
a mere peat floating in the Atlantic. What a triumph
it would have been if Lord Leverhulme had succeeded

BARRA, CASTLEBAY : KEISSIMUL CASTLE

where every one for hundreds of years, from the King down, had failed !

King James VI. determined to colonise Lewis— and it was perhaps his dry Scots humour that made him send a band of hard-headed Fifers to have a first try at taming the Macleod gentry.

It all began in 1597, when the Scots Parliament sitting in Edinburgh passed two Acts. The first Act ordained that all landlords, chieftains, leaders of clans, and others possessing or pretending rights to lands, should, by the 15th day of May 1598, produce their titles and find caution for payment of their future rents, failing which, they should be declared forfeited of all such lands. This was the beginning of the attempt to replace the chief's claymore with a lawyer's deed as a title to land. The second Act decreed the building of three burgh towns in the Highlands—one in Kintyre, another in Lochaber, and a third in Lewis. The King was to grant the sites and all privileges. We can well imagine how the warrior Macleods took these Parliamentary impertinences—for the principal forfeitures fell on Ruari and the whole clanjamfrey of his Macleod relatives—with the result that the Isle of Lewis-and-Harris was annexed to the Crown.

Then came the next act of the play—when eleven Fifeshire lairds and others formed themselves into a company to effect the "planting of policy" in Lewis. The eleven adventurers were Patrick, commendator of Lindores ; James Learmonth, of Balcomie ; Sir James Anstruther, younger of that ilk, Master of the Queen's Household ; James Spens, of Wormeston ; Sir James Sandilands, of Slamanno, Knight ; Captain William Murray ; John Forret of Fingask ; William, commendator of Pittenweem ; David Home, younger of

Wedderburn; Sir George Home, of Wedderburn, Knight, his father, administrator for him; and Ludovic, Duke of Lennox and Darnley. Their terms of contract with the Government were—That they should, at their own expense, " plant policy " in Lewis and in Trouterness, in Skye; that they should erect burghs of barony in Lewis, and four parish kirks there, with other two in Rona, Lewis; and that they should pay the King an annual rent, beginning with the first crop of 1600. So the contract was signed on 30th June 1598—a fine, easy thing for douce-dwelling Fifers or law-abiding Lowlanders to do. Then Dumbarton drums rolled out to the muster, and 500 or 600 volunteered as soldiers, while a number of artificers and labourers joined this grand jaunt to the Lewis to " plant policy "! The Fifer was a simple man, for once.

On 20th October 1598 the gallant fleet sailed from Fife, and, after an uneventful voyage, anchored near the grim Castle of Stornoway, which was then held by Murthow Macleod—not a brave mansion like the Castle we know so well to-day, which is a grey palace set amid little woodlands and green pleasaunces, but a bald, bare fortalice, with an ugly face and plenty of blood-stains in the dungeons. This was the first of three tries by the Fifers at " planting policy " in the Lewis.

But the Macleods were black affronted at the impertinence : the Mackenzies of Kintail were secret foes : and Macdonald of Sleat was already sharpening his dirk. A crop of claymores was the best harvest that the island had hitherto produced. The season was far advanced, but the Fife lairds were confident, so they ordered Murthow to surrender the fort. He refused. Then the 500 armed men attacked, and Murthow, with

NORTH UIST : ST CLEMENT'S CHURCH : VIEW FROM RODIL

his men, was compelled to take to the heather. But as he retreated he laughed to himself, well knowing that the fun was just beginning. This seemed such an easy victory to the Fifers that they thought the worst was over. Meantime Murthow, from his hiding-place on the vast moors, lay and watched. He left the Lewis weather to do the rest. The settlers had only been able to form a hasty camp where they landed stores. Then the island mists came down. The rains followed. The atmosphere was so raw and damp that swords and steel caps rusted in two or three days. In the melancholy world of soaking peat and bogs sickness began to spread among the colonists, and " through the coldness of the isle and the want of lodging and other entertainment, a number of them died of the flux." A dooms bad start was this.

A further supply of provisions for the winter was needed at once, and the laird of Balcomie agreed to return to Fife in his own ship. Balcomie was an ill man at the best. Had he not once so angered Andrew Melville at St Andrews that the sturdy Presbyter put a malediction on him ? Now, when his ship was not far gone on her voyage, imagine his chagrin when he saw a fleet of Highland birlinns—long eight-oared rowing-boats—closing in about his own little Fife vessel. It was Murthow and his Macleods! They straightway took the ship, murdered every one of the crew, but spared Balcomie, only to clap him into a secret dungeon in Lewis for six wintry months, all unknown to his Fife friends. The Fifers, in dool, began to build a pretty town. But poor Balcomie, sick and ill, very soon agreed to pay a ransom for his liberty, the money to be handed over only when he reached Fife. So the Macleods let him go, but he never saw the East Neuk again, for he took ill on the voyage and died on an Orkney isle.

Then these two grim brothers, Murthow and Neil Macleod, quarrelled, having no one at the moment but themselves to fight with. Although they were brothers by blood, Neil seized Murthow and a dozen of his friends. The dozen he murdered, but he kept Murthow for a worse fate. Hearing that the adventurers were open to negotiate, Neil Macleod said he would hand Murthow over to them, if they would obtain for himself the King's pardon and a portion of land in Lewis. The bargain was struck and Murthow was sent in chains to Edinburgh, guarded by a party under the lairds of Wormeston, Fingask, and Airdrie. And who is this that we see going with them ? Neil Macleod himself. Poor Murthow was taken to St Andrews, where, after being tried and condemned, he was executed. But what kind of luggage is this that Neil Macleod carried all the way to Auld Reekie ? A sack with the twelve bloody heads of his brother Murthow's friends in it as a present for King James ! Did ever a King get such a gruesome gift ?

Needless to say, Neil was an ill friend to the Fifers when they returned to Lewis, where their three chief objects of adventure were to cultivate the land, to develop the fisheries, and to civilise the natives. So when the laird of Wormeston set out on one occasion to kidnap the suspected Neil the crafty Lewisman waylaid the band on a sudden, and smote them so sorely that sixty were left dead and dying on the moors. It was now the autumn of 1601. If it needs a long spoon to sup with a Fifer the spoon had not yet been made that could sup with a Macleod, for the Lewis men next attacked the settlement of the colonists,

STORNOWAY : THE CASTLE ON THE LEFT

burned it to the ground, killed the soldiers, and dictated terms to the survivors. They were to leave the island never to return, to hand over all their rights to Tormod Macleod, to procure the royal pardon for the Macleods, and to leave the laird of Wormeston and his son-in-law, Thomas Monypenny of Kilkell, as hostages till the terms were ratified. These two sorry men had to thole the dungeons of Lewis for eight months before they saw Fife again. The Macleods, having no more Fifers to fight with, turned to claymore practice among themselves again. So ended the first try at colonising the isle of Lewis by the Fife adventurers.

Naturally the King and Council were wroth at the Macleods for flouting them with their blood-stained claymores; so on 19th June 1602 they proclaimed that the inhabitants of Lewis were " occupied in nothing else but in blood, murder, rief, theft, and oppression, every one of them exercising such beastly and monstrous cruelties upon others as have not been heard of amongst Turks and infidels "—and they added that the island was " the most fertile and commodious part of the whole realm, enriched with an incredible fertility of corn and plenty of fishes." The fishes were all there, but I fear the fertility of corn, like the gold dust of Martin's *Description*, was part of the Eldorado dream. A military muster was called again, and all the fencible men between sixteen and sixty in several of the northern shires were commanded to be ready by October of the same year. But the indignation of the Council cooled down, and at Falkland Palace the same Council determined, on 15th September, to postpone the expedition till the spring of 1603. By that time, as all the world knows, Queen Elizabeth, that royal lady of blessed memory, had died, and James VI., having been called south to the throne of England, forgot the wild men of Lewis in his new love for the glamorous realms of Merrie England—and thus Tormod and Neil Macleod were left in possession of the island.

But did the Fife lairds forget? No. They determined, after the lapse of two years, to make a second attempt at colonising Lewis. So in 1605 the Council, with a fine paper-fighting braggadocio, called the Macleods " an infamous byke of lawless limmers," and sent an expedition under Sir James Spens of Wormeston, Sir George Hay of Netherliff (afterwards Earl of Kinnoull and Chancellor of Scotland), and Sir Thomas Ker of Hirth, with every kind of documentary power, to employ fire and sword in reducing the Lewis limmers, calling on them to surrender to the King's officers within twenty-four hours. But the royal troops this time were absent! The adventurers, however, had gathered a military body of their own, and were accompanied by William Mac-Mhicsheumais, or Son of James, or Jamieson, Chief of the Clan Gunn. Tormod Macleod gave in on the promise of a trip to London to receive pardon from the King. But Neil—never! And how did it fall out? Tormod got his trip to London—the King was kind to him—but word soon came from the adventurers that Tormod would be better in Edinburgh Castle! So poor Tormod spent ten years in prison on the Rock of Auld Reekie, and when he did get out it was only on condition that he went to Holland and served the Prince of Orange. There he died—far from the Lewis of his heart, and

" The Hebrid Isles
Placed far amid the melancholy main."

It is a queer, mixed story.

Neil remained the irreconcilable fighting Celt. He kept the second batch of Fifers in a constant state of alarm by day and night. He was the bonny fighter and the beau-ideal of all the later types of Highland gentlemen of fortune, like Stevenson's Alan Breck. He was at home among his own hills and moors and sea-lochs. The Fife lairds once more grew sick of the ploy. So, after some of them had spent their fortune, they all shook their fists at Neil Macleod, and for the second time sailed for home. Neil Macleod, the *de facto* chief of the Seol Torquil, was once more king of the castle.

But if Highlanders are bonny fighters, Fifers are siccar souls. Lord Balmerino, Sir George Hay, and Sir James Spens agreed to make a third trial to colonise Lewis. Four years elapsed before the expedition set out, and by that time (1609) we know that Balmerino had fallen into deep disgrace for sending a letter to Pope Clement VIII., stamped with the King's signet, after James had refused to correspond with His Holiness. So Sir George Hay and Sir James Spens—bold men— took the third and last expedition into their own hands. This time they set out in summer. They had good support from armed auxiliaries, and, best (or worst) of all, the chief of Kintail was most friendly.

On disembarking at Stornoway without opposition, they found that they had not enough provisions for a long stay. The Chief of Kintail most politely offered to send a vessel from Ross-shire, full of provisions and chosen men, to help the adventurers in fighting Neil Macleod. But he did not mention that he had also sent a message to Neil telling him to intercept the vessel. This Neil promptly did—annexing the provisions, and thus starving the Fifers. There was nothing for it but to dismiss the Auxiliaries, and

B

Sir George Hay and Sir James Spens sailed for Fife themselves to get more food and help, leaving a weak and dispirited garrison behind them to defend the half-built town.

But men like Neil Macleod can see in the dark. So, one pitchy night, they swooped down on the settlement, set fire to the town, reduced the garrison, " burned and destroyed the whole victuals, furniture, insight, and plenishing, being within the said houses, to the value and estimation of £10,000 ; and at the same time most cruelly murdered and slew Patrick Giffert, servant to the Laird of Airdrie, with divers other servants and office men, within the said encampment."

Sir Walter Scott tells us that some old persons living in the Lewis about 1828 remembered " a very old woman living in their youth who used to say that she had held the lights while her countrymen were cutting the throats of the Fife adventurers." And then Sir Walter tells a creepy tale of the wife of one of the Fife gentlemen who fled to the wild morass of the Forest of Fannig, where she gave birth to a child, and was most mercifully cared for by a poor Hebridean man, who actually killed and disembowelled his own pony to give shelter within the carcass for the mother and new-born infant. Thus do the bitters and sweets of human life sit side by side with one another.

ISLE OF LEWIS : LOCH ROAG

III

THE ROCK OF BRISSAY

A ROBBER'S STRONGHOLD IN THE ATLANTIC

THIS is the story of the Rock of Brissay. Call it what you will—Birsay, Brissay, Berisay, or Bereasaidh—there it stands to-day, an outrageous islet in the Atlantic at the mouth of Loch Roag, on the west of Lewis, minding us of some long-forgotten Norse Viking, Beris, who called this little *ey* or island after his own name. From a distance, as Mackenzie says, it looks like a huge Saurian whose head has been chopped off, the head being the detached rock called *Stac an Tuill*—the Pillar of the Flood—which thrusts itself out of the water. In summer time, when the peace of heaven broods over the tranquil seas, Brissay sleeps in a dream of ethereal beauty—

> " Good is the smell of the brine that laves
>   Black rock and skerry,
> Where the great palm-leaved tangle waves
>   Down in the green depth,
> And round the craggy bluff pierced with caves
>   Seagulls are screaming."
>   —SHERIFF NICOLSON.

But in winter storm the mountainous seas roll across the Atlantic from the New World, terrific in their strength, and keep pounding on the walls of Brissay, then leap the rocks in a raging spume of spray when they are baffled. A Lewisman once said to me that the predominant note of his native seas is expressed in the one word *pounding*. So, in the wild, wet months Brissay stands like a stubborn giant that grows all the cleaner in his strength because the welter of ocean roars ceaselessly round the adamant walls.

Three hundred years ago Brissay was the robber-hold of that gallant rascal, our friend Neil Macleod.

He returned from Edinburgh to Lewis, and held the island for a time with his half-brother, Tormod. But the old blood feuds with the last of the Fife lairds soon broke out again, and as we have seen it was Tormod this time, with his hands tied behind his back to keep him out of mischief, who got a trip to London to see the King. From London he was sent back by the Wisest Fool in Christendom to Edinburgh Castle for safety! And there we leave him till the end of this tale.

Neil, the slippery one, remained the irreconcilable fighting islesman, until the Mackenzies of Kintail obtained possession of Lewis, and Neil was driven to take shelter as an outlaw on the sea-girt isle of Brissay. He was a wise strategist, for the little island is itself a natural fortress, which could be held by a handful of men against a multitude. Here, for nearly three years, Neil Macleod with thirty of his followers defied the Mackenzies. He had already stored the place with provisions, and when he needed more, a raid on the mainland of Lewis replenished his failing supplies.

One day the sentry reported that a rakish-looking ship was bearing down on Brissay with another ship in tow. Both ships then stood in for the land and anchored off the shores of Lewis. Neil, after a cautious reconnaissance, made himself known to the commander, who was one Captain Peter Love. His ship was the

Priam, a notorious English pirate ship. Her holds were stuffed with a rich cargo of sugar, cochineal, Barbary hides, some iron, and a number of muskets. The second ship was a prize which the *Priam* had at the end of a hawser. Here was a new enterprise for Neil Macleod and his merry men. So he struck up an acquaintance with the pirate Love, and offered to swear eternal friendship if only the sea-robber would agree to a co-partnership in piracy, with the Rock of Brissay for a stronghold and the good ship *Priam* for a guard. Love agreed. But Neil did not tell the pirate that his deliberate intention was to betray the whole gang into the hands of the Scottish Admiralty, that he himself might obtain new favour with the Government, and that his half-brother Tormod might be released from Edinburgh Castle. So, for a time, the English adventurer Love and Neil Macleod, the terror of Lewis, ranged the seas and raided the land to their hearts' content. Then—Neil calmly seized ship, cargo, and crew, and sent a letter to the Privy Council in Edinburgh offering to hand over Love, his ship and fellow-buccaneers, if only the Government would once more redress Neil's own particular grievances.

The Lords of Council were aghast at Neil's cool offer. They had been crying out for his blood but yesterday. Now, he had done good service to the King. So, having a great desire to settle the wearisome feuds in Lewis once and for all, the Lords sent a letter to Neil Macleod the Robber in which they told him that "whereas he has done very good service unto His Majesty and to the haill country . . . likeas, upon the assurance which we had of His Majesty's royal and princely regard in such cases, we will take upon us to assure him of His Majesty's pardon and favour."

B 2

But all was to depend on the delivery of the pirate ship, the captain, crew, and cargo.

So, on an October day the *Priam* was faithfully handed over by Neil to the Council's commissioner. Patrick Grieve, a skipper out of Burntisland, sailed north on a hired ship and took over the *Priam*. The pirate arrived at Leith in November, and on the 8th day of December Captain Love and seven of his sea-rovers were tried for piracy, were found guilty, and sentenced to be hanged on Leith sands within the flood-mark.

But Neil Macleod, who had betrayed poor Love and got him hanged, was well aware that others might betray him and have him hanged. So, acting on his own creed, he clung for safety to the Rock of Brissay, and tried to forget Tormod, who was languishing for a breath of the great north sea in a dungeon of Edinburgh Castle.

Now comes the last part of the story, which we owe to that eminent geographer and antiquary, but sometimes splairging historian, Sir Robert Gordon of Straloch and Pitlurg. The Mackenzies of Kintail determined to root out Neil and his robber band from Brissay. When it came to inventiveness in reprisals, one Highland clan was always as good as another, and the Tutor of Kintail gave orders that all the women and children belonging to Neil and his band were to be gathered together from their various homes on the mainland of Lewis. They were then rowed out and placed on a tidal rock near enough to Brissay for the Macleod robbers to see them and hear their cries when the tide came in. Neil was given this desperate choice —to surrender without condition, or to see his own wife and children and the women and children of his fellow-outlaws drowned by the tide which had now begun to lick the crowded rock. The robbers hesitated ; but the tide crept up. The women and children cried pitifully. The Mackenzies' hearts were as hard as Cruachan granite. At last, human nature and the love of kith and kin prevailed. Neil and his thirty thieves surrendered.

Perhaps it would not be worth our while to look for a tidal rock near Brissay to-day. Sufficient is it to know that Neil skulked in Harris for a time, gave himself up to Ruari Macleod, the Chief of Harris, begged him to take him to London to interview the King, and succeeded in persuading him to accede to his requests. But the Privy Council heard some sough of the travellers, stopped them at the town of Glasgow, and brought Neil to Edinburgh. There he was charged, on 30th March 1613, with the crimes of " fire-raising, burning, murder, and several thefts."

So, on a day in April Neil Macleod of Brissay was taken to the Market Cross of Edinburgh and there hanged upon a jibbet till he was dead, and thereafter his head was " strucken from his body " and affixed and set above the Nether Bow Port. So runs the sentence. Doubtless poor Tormod ground his teeth in the Castle dungeon because Neil had forgotten him, and he would have a queer sensation at the nape of the neck when the fatal moment came for Neil's rope collar to be fixed and his head struck off. But the Lord Advocate of that day—Sir Thomas Hamilton—writing to King James in London on 7th April, must have bit his crow quill several times, with a wry look on his face, before he wrote this epitaph of so unscrupulous a rascal—" Neil Macleod died at his execution very christianly."

IV

MULL OF THE MOUNTAINS

A GANGREL'S PARADISE

As we thrashed our way out from Oban one day after Easter, against wind and rain and tide, a remark of Rudolph, the Swiss guide, came to mind. He stood on the glacier in the midst of a torrential thunderstorm, and with an upward look at the clouds, said feelingly, " Can the good God not send down a little more rain ? " For, in this wild wet Western seaboard it had rained more or less for months ; and he who makes for Mull in a wet season is either deliberately asking for more, or is a hopeless optimist. But as we picked up the loom of Lismore through the driving mist and rain, and passed the Lady Rock, and sighted old Duart Castle on the nose of Mull, it was like returning home after many years of absence. In the drenching rain the old stories and legends came back to us one by one.

Lismore—the long green island which the wise old Gaelic name-makers called *Lios-more*, the great garden, where those *Episcopi Lismorienses*, the Bishops of Argyll, and that pioneer in Celtic literature, Dean Macgregor, once had their residence. The Lady Rock—that narrow reef, all foam-flecked now in the raging seas, where, three and a half centuries ago, a Maclean of Duart placed his wife at low tide, hoping to get rid of her when the flood came in. But she was a daughter of the Cailein More, the second Earl of Argyll; her brother rescued her, while the Maclean was glowering out of his window in Duart. Some time thereafter, having met his enemy in an eating-house in Auld Reekie, he stuck his Campbell dirk into the heart of the Duart murderer. Such is the story which the Lady Rock tells to every voyager up the Sound. Duart Castle itself has of late years been roofed in, and is now a Maclean residence once more. Old tales and old days—how they grip us still!

It seems but yesterday since we first sailed up the Sound of Mull, the most romantic Sound in the West —anchoring, year after year, in all its quiet bays— Craignure, Scallastle, Fishnish, Ardtornish—all of them full of happy memories, and most of them having a fine trout stream falling into the sea. Was it only in our dreams below deck, or actually standing on these shores before dawn, that we heard the sound of a forbidden splash net?

> " Sing me a song of a lad that is gone ;
> Say, could that lad be I ? "

But time wipes out all old scores. The sea birds are calling as of old on the Grey Rocks in mid-sound. At Ardtornish we miss the old house which used to stand behind the ruined castle. Here the Lords of the Isles held their parliaments and sang strange sea-chanties after their feastings in the hall. The rain, however, takes off as we slow down at Salen Pier, and with one bundle (not to speak of the bagpipes) on the back and another on the bicycle a solitary stravaiger steps ashore, with an inward chuckle of delight, on *Muile nam Mor-bheann*—Mull of the Great Bens— happy to be back on this island of the heart with a new road stretching before him every morning, and the world for his pillow every night.

Mull for its size is an island of vast variety. Turning its almost unbroken back on Morven across the Sound, it thrusts great arms into the Atlantic. At its narrowest waist, from Salen on the Sound to Loch-na-Keal it is only four miles across. Indeed the Atlantic has bitten so deeply into Mull of the many sea lochs that the island has a coastline of 300 miles. Being entirely volcanic the shores are rocky and precipitous, with cliffs a thousand feet high, and stretches of fine white sand at such places as Calgary, the Ross, and the Sound of Iona. Ben More, Ben Talaidh, and Dun da Ghaoithe dominate the island. Here and there, at Loch Spelve, Craignure, and about the head of Loch-na-Keal, one may wander in woodlands thickly planted. But, for the rest, it is literally *Tir nam Beann, s'nan Gleann, s'nan Gaisgeach*—the Land of Hills and Glens and Heroes.

Let a wandering man loose on Mull, and he will find it a gangrel's paradise. With Salen as a centre he may make his way up the Sound past Aros to Tobermory, or down the Sound to Duart. He may cut through the long glen of Aros, by Loch Frisa, on the right-hand to Dervaig, in the north, or take the way by Loch-na-Keal and the mighty Gribun cliffs to Kinloch Inn at the head of Loch Scridain. He will then return eastward by the Great Glen to Loch Spelve and Duart; or better still, he will continue his pilgrimage by Bunessan, along the bare granite Ross of Mull to Fionphort, and cross the narrow Sound of Iona to worship at Columba's shrine. But, one way or another, wherever he goes he will have a glamorous outgait to the west, with islands everywhere on his horizon—

SOUND OF IONA : REEFS AND ISLETS OFF ERRAID

Eorsa, Ulva, and Gometra, Inchkenneth, Little Colonsay, Staffa of the columns and caves, and farther out, the lonely Treshnish Isles, Fladda, Lunga, and the Dutchman's Cap, with the two Cairn-na-Burgs lying like islands of the blessed in the sunset light of the broad Atlantic.

The holiest place in Scotland belongs to Mull—Iona. All the world may buy a guide-book to the namely relics of Columba's Isle. But only love, memory, knowledge, and the mystic's vision can unlock the secret of this Isle of Dream. The spirit of Columba, that Saint of blessed memory and martial monk with the tender heart, still broods over the green machaii lands, the old grey stones, and the pure white sands. Yonder the dreamer may see the holy men landing from the coracles at the little bay—that navy of heaven which brought from Ireland more wealth of Christ than all the greatest ships of war. Here were set up the little cells, the wattled huts, the tiny thatch-and-timber church, the grinding mill. By the shores of this iridescent strait, whose waters gleam in the sunlight with heavenly greens and blues, opals and amethysts, Columba spoke to the fishes of the sea. On a wintry morning he saw a vision of God's love as he threw crumbs to the starving birds, and when they flew away he cried, "Oh, little birds—if only you knew the thoughts and feelings of Columba's heart towards you, you would not have taken fright!" The street of the dead, the silent crosses, the four-square church, the limitless seas—how long it seems since these sands of Hy were drenched with the blood of the martyred monks by the fair-haired vikings who for 400 years ruled these Western Isles! And yet, as we sit alone and dream, the very winds that blow about the graves become Columba's voice calling us to worship God.

Bunessan and Loch Lathaich call up another memory of a midsummer night and a white-winged schooner becalmed on the glassy sea, away out by the Treshnish Isles. All through the windless night the long low Atlantic swell made thunder in the distant caves of Staffa and on the cliffs of Mull. For the bosom of the Atlantic heaves even when the great sea seems asleep. The stilly night was made eerie by the pitiful calling of the seamews and the unearthly laughter of the puffins. Slowly but surely, the tides were drifting us nearer the rocks of Staffa. Then, a radiance appeared behind the great hills of Mull, putting out the stars one by one. A long black line began to steal over the sea, out of the very mouth of morning. It was the wind of dawn—that miracle of nature which is begotten so mysteriously in the chilly hour of daybreak. Nearer and nearer it came, this unseen spirit of deliverance, whose hissing steps made black the sea of glass—and, in a moment, the wind struck the sails of the motionless yacht like the clap of a hand. She heeled over to the very rail, and soon was flying for Bunessan like a frightened ghost. The sun came up behind the wild cliffs of Gribun with a thousand angry lights, that spread great streaks of blood-red glory in the east. The very waters borrowed the colour from the morning skies, and we were rushing through a sea that seemed to leap with blood. And yet, when at last the anchor went out with a rattle in the quiet loch, the wind died away as mysteriously as it had come, and we stood on deck and watched the seals basking on the weedy rocks in the warm silence of the new-born day.

That is the charm of Mull. You may begin the

day in torrents of rain, and yet be taking your lunch on a rock with the sun drying your dripping clothes. The skies may seem leaden and hopeless, but when they break the blue is ethereal, and the islands glitter green and grey on the surface of a sapphire sea. It was exactly so one day when I crossed from Salen to Loch-na-Keal under the dreary drip of most depressing rain clouds. And yet, by midday, when searching for the foundations of an old chapel in a wood near Kellan, the wet earth was blushing green in the sunlight, the primroses were starring the russet carpet of the woods, the blue glitter of the loch was seen through a veil of grey hazel twigs, and a stone's-throw from where I stood, breathing in the delicious breath of spring, the brown tents of the wandering folks were set beneath the trees, where the children of the homeless clan ran wild.

Mull is full of ancient graveyards, and the search after carved Celtic stones is an adventure which only a keen antiquary can ever understand. Beauty lurks in the most unexpected places. Standing within the walls of an old ruin like the chapel of Pennygown, or exposed to all the wind and rain on a high-set knoll at Dervaig, or hidden away beneath the immemorial turf which has to be patiently removed—the great reward comes to him who seeks and searches alone. At Gruline there is a standing-stone in the middle of an open field. On wandering across the field to sketch this stone, I suddenly became aware of three Highland children yelling in great alarm from the gate behind me. They were warning me about a mad bull. I had, indeed, noticed marks of terrific hoofing in the mud at the gate as I passed through. Now, I saw the bull eyeing me beyond the standing-stone, and the furious yelling of

the children did not help to pacify his majesty of the
great horns. But the stone had to be sketched, so,
with one eye on the stone, another on the bull, and
both ears open to the children's cries, the work was
quickly done, and a safe retreat accomplished.

There are silent God's acres everywhere—on
Gometra, on Inchkenneth, at Carsaig, Dervaig,
Glengorm, in Glen Aros and Glen Forsa, at Knock
on Loch-na-Keal, at Loch Buie, at Garmony, and at
Pennygown. Not ordinary grave enclosures, but
ancient burial-grounds, centuries old. Of all the
romantic spots where the dead sleep in Mull (apart
from Iona) give me Pennygown. This ancient place
of graves stands on a broad, flat plain of close-cropped
turf above the Sound, and the ruined chapel of Pennygown stands within the black kirkyard walls. Rough
steps lead up to the top of the wall, and the green
howes are rounded with the finest sea-grass. Here is a
warrior's effigy stone—doubtless a great Maclean—all
weather-worn now, but still showing a sword in one
hand and a dirk in the other. Beside him on the turf
lies an effigy of his wife. The chapel walls are almost
intact, with the little rounded arches of the windows
all worn away. Near the ambry in the east wall stands
a priceless Celtic stone, with the head of the cross
broken off. But what remains is beautiful. On the
one side is a flowing circular design ending in the tail
of a couching griffin, and beneath that a full-sailed
galley. On the other side there is an elaborate carving
of the Virgin and Child, with more Celtic tracery, and
the remains of an inscription below.

While I was standing in the twilight within the
roofless chapel of Pennygown sketching this stone the
wind moaned through the broken windows, and the

Bridge of Orchy and River

long-lost memories of the sleepers came to life again as the warm rain smirred the dying light of day.

Next morning April leaped on Mull like a tiger, and Pennygown was basking in the sun. The waters of the Sound were glittering under a blue sky, and the grassy plain by the sea was as brilliant as an emerald. Opposite, on the Morven coast, was Fiunary, that haunted place of song and story, where, long ago, the High Priest of Morven kept *ceilidh* in the manse kitchen, and of which the great Norman wrote his sweet " Farewell to Fiunary." Perhaps there never has been a Highland family in Scotland that gave so much to the Kirk in feet and inches, as well as in good, godly human nature, as the Macleods of Morven. How pleasant to me are my memories of Fiunary! Lying becalmed in that sunset Sound, dreaming long dreams of Gaelic men and old-time things ; the glassy waters all golden-washed in the summer twilight ; the sound of music floating from a motionless barque where the foreign sailors were singing their strange chanties ; the lonely manse of the Macleods standing above the green woods of Fiunary, all glamorous in the lambent light. Now, on the sunlit shore below the green graves, the pipes send a lament for the dead in Pennygown across the water to the dead in Fiunary, with a march of battle for the Macleans who fought here long ago in a deadly feud, from which there rode away a headless horseman.

There is somewhere in Mull—where exactly I have not yet found out—a little burial-ground entirely devoted to unbaptised children, who were thus, according to the harsh theology of the Kirk, severed in the grave from those who had been well-happed in the hope of resurrection to eternal life. Only one adult lies with the little babes—an old Christian woman,

whose last request was that she should be buried with
the unbaptised children. So the unblessed babes
found a mother in death, when the old *cailleach* came
to them with her virgin heart full of love.

The road from Tobermory to Dervaig is the steepest
in Mull. Just above this little town of Mary's Well
another road branches to the right and leads to Castle
Gorm, that stately pile which looks right across the
seas past Ardnamurchan to Coll and Rhum and Eigg
and Skye. Along this road there is a field which still
flashes upon the inward eye, for it used to be as white
as driven snow with marguerites in the month of June.
The Dervaig road rises 500 feet from the sea-level,
reaches its summit at the Mishnish Lochs, then descends
for four miles in a series of hairpin bends, which are
not soon forgotten. But the glory of the backward
view to Ben Hiant and Ben Resipol far up Loch Sunart,
the utter loneliness of the moors of Mull in the evening
twilight, and the sharp hungry air were more than
reward for this nine miles up and down hill. Some
weeks before about forty wild swans made their way
from Iceland or Siberia to Loch Cuin—and on passing
the Mishnish Lochs I saw fifteen of these snow-
white visitors, with three others in little Loch-an-Torr
farther on.

At the foot of the last hill lies Dervaig, a quaint
little village of one street, which stands at the head of
Loch Cuin. I have moving memories of my last visit
to this village many years ago, when, having drifted in
windless weather for three days and nights from Skye
to Mull, we anchored far out in Loch Cuin, almost
foodless, at one o'clock in the morning, and had to
walk two miles to buy the wherewithal for breakfast.

Near Dervaig, on a high knoll above the road,

Loch Linnhe : View at Kentallen

stands the old graveyard, where the pre-Reformation church may still be traced among the graves. It was a clear, windy day when I took rubbings of a Celtic cross which lies prone on the turf. The shaft must have lain exposed to the weather for generations. Both sides are beautifully carved. On the top there is a crucifixion, with what seems to be a representation of the two malefactors. At the foot of the shaft there is a pair of shears, marking the stone as a memorial to a priest—for the shears were a symbol of the tonsure. The under side of the stone shaft had not been exposed for a very long time, with the result that on turning it over we found the carving perfectly embossed on the hard earth, like a beautiful squeezing. The fine three-circled head of this cross has long ago been broken off. Quite close by there is another carved stone, greatly worn with feet and weather. Both of these stones are of slaty schist, and have evidently been brought from another island or district where that kind of rock must have been common.

From the commanding site of this old burial-ground a magnificent view can be had of the whole Dervaig valley seawards. The present parish church, restored after the true old Celtic style, stands near the village, with a wholly appropriate round tower attached. Quinish, Penmore, Calgary, and Kilninian are all reached from Dervaig.

Here my last and best days in Mull were spent. On Sunday morning we sat in the dim stone church, with the white cloths spread on the Communion tables. A namely gospeller from Gigha, who is a rare collector of Celtic songs, a poet, and a true mystic, spoke of Columba and of the Great Sacrifice in language of haunting beauty.

At Torr-a-chlachan I had often need to sing this *Rune of Hospitality* from the isle of Eigg :—

> " I saw a stranger yestreen ;
> I put food in the eating place,
> Drink in the drinking place,
> Music in the listening place ;
> In the sacred name of the Triune ;
> He blessed myself and my house,
> My cattle and my dear ones ;
> And the lark said in her song,
>   Often, often, often
> Goes the Christ in the stranger's guise,
>   Often, often, often
> Goes the Christ in the stranger's guise."
>
> *Translation by* KENNETH MACLEOD.

On the Monday morning at four o'clock, when the hills were still wrapped in the robe of night, this Gaelic old word sounded in the ear of the stranger as he rose to take his departure :—

> " A soft path for the far traveller,
>   A soft path for the far traveller."

Within the hour, having supped with those whose best gift is kindness, there was nothing for it but to say "The Smooring Blessing" of the Hebrid Isles, and be gone :—

> " Blest be this house, blest be this fire,
> And blest be this people all.
>   .   .   .   .   .
> An angel in the door of every room,
> To shield and to protect you all
> Till bright daylight comes in the morning."
>
> *From* " Carmina Gadelica."

Then, the bundle was swung on the back, the lamp of friendship shone out in the darkness, and the foot went up the old road for the hills again, under the glitter of a thousand stars.

V

THE BAD STEP

A JACOBITE HIDIE HOLE IN THE ORKNEYS

THE Bad Step is the mischancy name that is usually
applied to an awkward bit on the shore track round
Loch Scavaig, in Skye. This track leads from Camu-
sunary to the far-famed fresh-water loch of Coruisk
which lies in a gloomy cup of the Coolins—surely the
weirdest bit of fresh-water in Scotland or on the Isles.
But there is another Bad Step in the Ultima Thule of
the ancients, which is not readily forgotten by those
who have crept along the cliff-face ledge that leads to
the Gentlemen's Cave in the island of Westray.

Westray and North Ronaldsay are the most northerly
islands of the Orkneys, lying far removed amid the
melancholy main. Here you are in an atmosphere
which is neither Scots nor Highland, for the Orcadians
pride themselves on their Scandinavian ancestry, and
are as far removed from the Gaelic-speaking Celts of
Sutherland as the twang of a Kirkwall man is from the
lilting speech of a Selkirk souter. Round these far isles
the vikings sailed for centuries, and there to-day you
can hear the sound of the sea-waves rising and falling
in the isleman's tongue.

To thrash through the racing tides from island to
island for a whole day on a little coasting steamer that
carries cattle and sheep, provisions and passengers, is

to be like a salted herring when the darkness falls. For the spindrift and the rain fly mingled together over these North Sea isles, where the smell of fish is as the breath of life. But the Orkneys are so full of antiquarian lore that the digger into ancient things will gladly go the round of the islands on any pretext to feed his soul on legends and tales, Picts' houses and ruined brochs, Maeshowe and the Stones of Stennis, old kirks and bald grey castles.

It was long ago. But on my way to Westray I made the circle of the islands, and came off at the little island of Eday to spend the week-end. The boat drew into a bay behind the Calf of Eday, and we landed in a wet October twilight. A drive of three and a half miles right down the centre of this narrow isle brought me to a hospitable house in the heather, where I found a warm welcome. Next day, being Sunday, I was a free man for a couple of hours in the afternoon. Accordingly, I mapped out an excursion to some antiquities in Eday, particularly an underground dwelling on a little hill close by.

But—

> " The best laid schemes o' mice and men
>   Gang aft agley."

For, there was a baby in the house, and the fond young mother said it would go to no one ! That was a challenge which any child lover would have accepted. So the dear lady, taking advantage of an innocent remark, paid me the embarrassing compliment of leaving her first-born with me for the whole afternoon. With my heart in the ancient things of the world outby, I was tethered to the newest thing in the world at the study fire, till the gloaming fell. As I had to leave in the dark next morning, the Picts' House of Eday will remain to the end of time a lost adventure.

But I found no babies in Westray. Only a beadle who, on my remarking how cold the church must be in winter without any means of heating, glared at me— after service—with a contemptuous eye, and said, " Young man, we heat this kirk frae the pulpit ! "

The late October days went by all too soon. I can still see the little Bay of Pierowall, with its tiny circle of houses looking across the sea to Papa Westray, two or three miles away. Every road was explored, from Rapness to Noup Head, from Inga Ness to Rap Wick. But the glamour of Westray for me lay to the west, past Noltland Castle, to the wild wall of cliffs and rocks which runs from Noup Head to Inga Ness. Here the little Westray hills, none of them over 600 feet—North Hill, Couter's Hill, Knucker Hill, Gallow Hill, Fitty Hill, and Skea Hill—look right into the eye of the sunset, like sentinels, as the great red ball of fire goes down beyond the rim of the tumbling seas. The very names of the rocks and creeks and bays are reminiscent of the vikings and their high sea gests—Kelda Ber, Hark Lone, Starry Geo, Red Nev, and Mirky Hole.

And the Castle of Noltland—that ruin which Billings called the most northerly building of architectural interest in Britain—how the old tales come ringing down the centuries as one stands before an old castle and marks the crumbling glories of its founds and walls. It was built by Thomas de Tulloch, Bishop of Orkney and Governor of the Isles under Eric of Denmark, some time between 1422 and 1448. There was a stone in Billings's time with the builder's initials, " T. T.," on it, and the figure of a kneeling bishop. But that stone and many others are now gone. Adam

Bothwell, Bishop of Orkney, conveyed Noltland to his brother-in-law Gilbert Balfour of Westray, the Master of Queen Mary's Household, and Captain of Kirkwall Castle in 1560. It was this Adam Bothwell who was Commendator of Holyrood. He performed the Protestant marriage between Queen Mary and his own cousin, the notorious Bothwell, who is described in the marriage contract as " the right noble and potent Prince, James Duke of Orkney, Earl Bothwell, Lord Hailes, Crichton, and Liddesdale, Great Admiral of this Realm of Scotland." It was Adam Bothwell's daughter, too, who was commemorated in the haunting ballade called " Lady Anne Bothwell's Lament." She was loved and betrayed by her own cousin, the Hon. Alexander Erskine, brother of the Earl of Mar. After being deserted, she sang her tragedy into this lullaby or lament or baloo as it is variously called, while, with a broken heart, she rocked her innocent babe in the cradle :—

> " Baloo, my babe, lie still and sleep,
>   It grieves me sair to see thee weep,
>   If thou be silent I'll be glad,
>   Thy moaning makes my heart full sad.
>
> " Baloo, my boy, weep not for me,
>   Whose greatest grief is wronging thee ;
>   Nor pity her deserving smart
>   Who can blame none but her fond heart."

What memories of love and dool, what old tales from the deeps of time keep soughing round the walls of many a ruined castle in Scotland and the Isles, as the twilight winds moan through its empty windows and about its crumbling turrets ! It is even said that Noltland was intended to be an asylum for the hapless Queen. Balfour indeed paid dear for his loyalty to his

Royal mistress, for he forfeited the estate in 1571, and died in the service of Eric XIV. of Sweden. Failing issue through his son, the restored estate passed to his cousin-german, Sir Michael Balfour, and in Sir Michael's time Noltland suffered a siege. Here, too, some of Montrose's officers found refuge after defeat at Carbisdale in the Kyle of Sutherland. But Cromwell had a long memory, and poor Balfour, for keeping company with the Cavaliers, had to fly to Holland. Then came the Jacobite Rising of 1745, when William Balfour of Trenabie, like many another gallant Jacobite laird, drew down upon him the anger of the Hanoverians. The Castle of Noltland was then burned, never to be rebuilt. It was at this time that Balfour and his friends were compelled to skulk in caves and dens of the earth.

A gey race were these same Balfours. Indeed, it is told of one of them, that he had thirty-six children, and stood six feet seven inches in height. At the marriage of one of his daughters he kept open house, like a King of Thule, for four months. At long last the greedy guests went home, but not until the last joint had been eaten from the last beast, and that the bull !

This brings us to the Bad Step and the Jacobite Hidie Hole.

Leaving Noltland Castle and taking the road to a little farm which stands nearest to the cliffs, I set out one day to find the path along the cliff-face to the Gentlemen's Cave. But nature never designed that road for a promenade of pleasure. Having failed to find it, I returned to the farm, and an old man, who was himself a cragsman, came with me as guide. Soon we were on the ledge which led us right along the face of the cliff. A wall of solid rock rose above us, and

there was a drop of eighty feet to the sea, which boiled
and grumbled in yeasty foam against the cliff-foot
below. The cliffs here are nearly 200 feet high, the
contour line just sweeping the grassy base of the North
Hill, which slopes to the giddy edge. It was comparatively easy going for one who was accustomed to
great heights and had a steady climber's head.

But soon the old man stopped.

" Take off your shoes, now, and do exactly what
I do."

For the ledge had come to an abrupt end, and I felt
a trickle of uneasiness as I looked past him and saw
that there was a gap with a rough, V-shaped void cut
right into the wall of the cliff. It was the Bad Step.

The old man took off his shoes. Then he deliberately sat with his legs dangling over the end of the
ledge. He next felt with his right foot for a rock-hold
on the cliff-face, and when he had found it he reached
up to another hold for his right hand on the cliff-face
above him. Then he took a delightfully easy spring
across and landed on the farther side of the gap. Standing up, he gave his next order.

" Now sit down. Put your right foot down there
and your right hand up here, and step across."

He said it as coolly as a butler might open a drawing-
room door and request you to step in.

I sat down. For a moment I saw the sea boiling
between my legs eighty feet below as I stretched my
right foot out to the hold. But looking up for the
hand-hold had a steadying effect, and, having got both,
I took the spring and landed beside the old man.

" Some folk whiles come here to see the cave,"
said my companion with calm indifference, " but—
they never win ower. It is a Bad Step."

We then walked in our stockings down the ledge, which gradually slanted seawards, until we came to the caves. The sea broke in spray over the rocks as we stood and thought of William Balfour, Stewart of Brough, and the other ten Jacobite gentlemen who lived here for a whole winter, not daring to light a fire. Food was brought to them by an old man. There was certainly no danger of a stranger strolling along the cliff face. The Bad Step was both their danger and their safety. In the inner cave they would be more sheltered from the weather. From the sea none could surprise them. Their only companions were the screaming seabirds. To the infinite West the ocean stretched from their very feet. The waves made a perpetual diapason in these solid rocky halls. It was a complete, if a miserable place of refuge.

Then I remembered the Virgilian phrase of cold comfort—

" Facilis descensus Averno—sed ! "

So we retraced our steps up the ledge until we came again to the gap. It is one thing to do a risky thing once, before the knowledge of its difficulty has sunk into the imagination. But it is quite another thing to repeat it with the recollection of its risk filling the mind with ugly apprehensions. It is also easier to take a climber's risk with the right hand and right foot, than with the less proficient left hand and left foot. But the old man, like a wise man, left no time for thought or remark. No rope bound us together for moral support. When he sat down and took the left-hand spring across the gap there was nothing for it but to do the same. Doubtless an expert rock climber would think nothing of it. But to this day I feel a slight sinking in the region of the stomach when I recall the waves breaking eighty feet below. So it was a happier man who sat down on the other side and laced his shoes.

Since then I have seen many a Jacobite hidie hole in Scotland—in the Outer Hebrid Isles ; in caves on mountain sides of the mainland ; behind the arras in the drawing-room of one of the oldest and quaintest mansions in Scotland, where a piano now stands against the innocent-looking tapestry, and a cradle of James VI. once rocked by Queen Mary's hand, stands in the middle of the floor. We honour the men who suffered such privations and took such risks for *Tearlach Og*. But never did I realise more what risky lodgings they occupied than when creeping along the ledge of the cliff-face to the Gentlemen's Cave in Westray. It was a Bad Step, and no mistake.

VI

THE COMING OF SPRING

ON THE BRAES OF PERTHSHIRE

WITH the coming of spring all tramps grow restless, and one by one the gangrels of the road throw the bundle on the back and take the glamorous way that leads out of the city to the northlands or the southlands, as each thinks best. Whether it be in a garden or in a heart, it is there—the upward urge, the life thrill, the mystic push of spring, which means flowers in the poorest garden and hopes in the oldest heart. Now is the time when many a lusty fellow throws the drones over his shoulder, takes the world for his pillow, and steps out bravely to the tune of " Bundle and go " on the old highway that has something new round every corner. The wine of April sends the blood dancing through the veins like fire. Winter is over. The sun shines out of the blue-white skies. The rain showers fall soft and sweet, like heavenly kisses, on the upturned earth. The little blood-red buds of spring are everywhere. The bird's song calls forth the heart's song, as the tramp goes singing down the lanes with a laugh at those poor dependants who wrap themselves in furs and cultivate liverish sorrows in splendid cars. For who is so master of his circumstance as the strong man, with the love of a free life in his heart ? So, with a stick birling in his hand, he swings along the road, with no programme but whatever comes next in the day's adventure :—

> There's a gangrel bit in the heart of me
>   That makes me sib to the wandering man,
> And many a time has my soul cried out
>   For the way men lived when the world began—
> Wind, and sun, and the splash of rain,
>   And the bonny brown earth to roam ;
> With beasts and birds and flowers for friends,
>   And the bield of a wood for home.

To me April comes never more sweetly than in the glades and glens of Perthshire. The face of a countryside is like the face of a friend—plain or beautiful, it takes a lifetime to know it, and even then the true lover is lost for language. So have I, many times, taken the road round the Knock at Crieff and, dreaming in the sun, over the rail of the wooden bridge that crosses the limpid Shaggie Burn, on my way to the old, familiar glen. And yet—these green haughs, these deep-gladed woods, the smell of the pines, and the thunder of the waterfalls on a sunny April day seem liker a miracle of God than ever.

On this road the towny traveller usually sits down to rest himself beside his beloved on an iron seat below the Barvick Falls, before returning to the midday meal at home, that intolerable tyranny which no true tramp can abide. But, for the wandering man, the day's adventure is just beginning, so he climbs up the right bank of the stream above the waterfall, finding his way through the sludgy loam of the woods, clambering over fallen trees, and peering down into the gorge where the river tumbles headlong in many a white waterfall. It is a stey path till you reach the highest fall, and come to a little old greystone bridge that crosses this moorland stream where it enters the wood. Here you will find an idyllic seat on the parapet as you look towards the brown hills and listen to the whaups.

> " What thochts o' the lang grey moorland
>   Start up when I hear that cry !
> The times we lay on the heather
>   At the well, lang syne gane dry ;
> And aye as we spak' o' the ferlies
>   That happened afore time there,
> The whaup's lone cry on the win' cam' by
>   Like a wild thing tint in the air.
>
> " And though I ha'e seen mair ferlies
>   Than grew in the fancy then,
> And the gowden gleam o' the boyish dream
>   Has slipp'd frae my soberer brain,
> Yet—even yet—if I wander
>   Alane on the moorland hill
> That queer wild cry frae the gurly sky
>   Can tirl my heart strings still."
>   —ROBERT WANLOCK REID.

The gloomy Blue Craigs (2535 feet) encircle the glenhead, where fields of winter snow still lie dazzling white against the blue April sky. On these snowfields beyond the Blue Craigs I have found in early spring a dead frog frozen stiff, having only had strength to travel half-way across the level snow, which was many feet deep. Who can tell the vagaries of frogs ? For I have had letters from the Himalayas and from the Andes telling me of the antics of frogs in snowfields at very high altitudes.

But our way to-day lies down the outside of the wood again to the Glen road and over the bridge near the sawmill. Every turn of these mossy paths through the Ochtertyre woods is familiar—in snow and frost, in spring and autumn, when the larches hang out their first delicate green tassels, and when the deep glades and avenues of ancient trees glow red and gold and russet with every colour of autumn. Beautiful for situation is Ochtertyre, that old Scots house whose eyes are continually winking in the sun, and whose policies are steeped in sunshine the livelong summer days. Ochtertyre always reminds me of David Livingstone's description of the grave of Mary Moffat, his wife, in the heart of Africa, by the large baobab-tree on the hill at Shupanga—"Mary sleeps on Shupanga's brae, beeking fornent the sun." That is Ochtertyre. High set, against the bieldy woodlands, it looks down on the most natural of lakes, beeking fornent the sun.

There is a certain huge Scots fir, with a red arm bending upward over a path. Here, sitting one day alone in the heat and silence, I picked up a large fir cone, and in an act of nature worship broke it suddenly open. The imprisoned breath of spring was released, like a whiff of woodland incense. These woods at dawn are full of bird music. Here, later on, the cuckoo haunts the hills with its wandering voice. The little brown squirrels run wild. Flowers star the pathways— primroses, anemones, hyacinths—and always the sound of falling water fills the glades of Turret with a delicious husheen.

On a flat bluff of rock overlooking the deep linn of the Falls there is a seat. You look right down the little valley to the distant hills of Ochill. To me, in early spring, it is the Valley of the Purple Mist. For just before the trees break into greenery the tangle of a million twigs in this wooded gorge of the river makes a transparent mist of purple grey, delicate, elusive, and far more beautiful than all the later leafage of the summer woods. Behind the seat a mass of red osiers fills a lush hollow by the path, making a crimson glow beneath the trees. Such are the early beauties of these glades and glens—purple mist in the valley and crimson fire in a dingle of the wood.

How many come here to look at the Falls from yon hollow grotto in the depths without knowing the story of the Toshach and the Fairy! Long ago, when the castle of Monzievaird stood on the hill, the last Toshach of Monzievaird, or readman of the King, used to leave his castle and make his way down to these Falls of Turret. Here he met the beautiful fairy who haunted the glen. He fell desperately in love with her, and was seldom away from the leafy valley of the river. At last his wife, suspecting something more than mere nature-worship, followed the Toshach, and saw him making love to the fairy. The fairy fled, the wife in a huff went home to her father's halls, and

" The sun of Toshach set to rise no more."

To those who know these Turret and Barvick hills the cairn on the top of Achinochen Hill must be a familiar object on the skyline. That is Kenneth's Cairn —a huge pile of stones raised in remembrance of Kenneth III., who in 1005 was slain in battle on the plain of Monzievaird fighting against Malcolm II., the true heir to the Crown of Scotland. From Kenneth's Cairn there is a way down into Glenalmond by the Kirk of the Grove and the Eagle's Rock. But the spring comes late on these Turret heights and on Ben Chonzie (3045 feet) at the very head of the glen.

It was from this hill that the Duke of Atholl, as
King of Man, obtained the pair of falcons which he
presented as a hereditary tribute to King George III.
on his Coronation. For the Dukes of Atholl were not
only lords of that ilk, but for a long time (1775-1829)
they were Kings of Man as well. The second Duke
obtained this sovereignty through his descent from the
youngest daughter of the seventh Earl of Derby, whose
family had for centuries held the Kingship of Man
from the Crown. Parliament purchased the Sovereignty
of Man in 1765 for £70,000 and an annuity of £2000
a year, the Duke retaining certain rights of the manor
and the gift of patronage. But the last remaining
interests of the Atholl family in the Isle of Man were
transferred to the British Crown in 1829. On this
same hill of Ben Chonzie the last wolves in Scotland
are said to have been slain. Eagles used to nest in this
neighbourhood, but of their presence now I have no
personal knowledge.

Those who wander on to the Knock at Crieff will
see one of the finest panoramas in Scotland. Far to
the west Ben Voirlich lifts his pearly peak into the
blue, and all between there lies a country of hills and
rivers, woodlands and glens, from Loch Earn to your
feet. Dr John Brown once called this the finest twenty
miles of scenery in Scotland. To tell the story of that
twenty miles—Ardvorlich, Dunira, Aberuchill, Lawers,
Strowan, Drummond, Ochtertyre, and Monzie—with
Prince Charlie at Ferntower down-by, and the town of
Crieff for a feud centre, would be to tell the whole
history of the clash and clang of the Scots clans, with
legends enough to stock a library. Did not the Stewards
of Strathearn, that royal race, hold a court at Crieff as
early as 1218? Was it not in this same town that the

Dunkeld Abbey : The Parent Larches

" Kind gallows of Crieff " stood, before which the wild
Highlanders used to touch their bonnets and say—
" God bless her nainsel and the teil tamn you " ?
But Sir Walter was as little a Highlander as the words
which he ascribed to his Highland robbers were good
Gaelic. Before descending, however, from the Knock,
it is worth while to remember that at this spot, high
above Monzie, where the path ends, one of the last
witches in Scotland was burned in 1715. A mischancy
queyn was this witch of Monzie—Kate M'Niven. She
was nurse to the family of Inchbrakie, and had tried to
poison her foster-son, Patrick, the laird. Such were
her powers of evil that she could on occasion turn
herself into a bee, and then she went buzzing about on
her errands of black magic. The minister of Monzie
was bitter against her, and the Presbytery of Auchter-
arder condemned her to be burnt at the stake. Not
even Patrick Graeme, her foster-son, could save the
poor woman. So she was tied to a tree and burned
here at the path-end. In her death agony she bit a
stone from her necklace, and spat it towards Patrick
Graeme. An uncut sapphire—this stone was set in a
ring which was afterwards kept in the family of Inchbrakie as a charm.

Poor Kate M'Niven has been dead these two
hundred years and more, and the cuckoo is calling us
to take the road through the wood of Monzie. The
great grey castle stands on the green, with a little modest
bit of original Scots domestic building at the side of
the later stately pile. These tall old larch-trees which
rise from the gardens by the lake were originally brought
here by Menzies of Culdares. He presented similar
specimens to the Duke at Dunkeld about 160 years
ago. So the larches at Meggernie in Glenlyon, at

D

Dunkeld, and at Monzie are claimed to be among the oldest in Scotland.

But the wandering man avoids castles, so we cross the avenue, pass over the beech-tree heights, and so reach the road beyond the three ponds—the haunt of the heron—just where the Kelty Burn comes tumbling through a grey coppice. In the primrose time of the year, you will find the brown tents of the homeless folk and the blue reek of gipsy fires rising from the banks of the stream. But to-day the fires are black out, and the brown-faced children of Little Egypt are not here to pull the catkins which have burst into golden showers of fairy rain. Is any carpet on earth to be compared with the russet rug of leaves which Mother Nature throws down in the vaulted rooms of the forest? This wide mossy mountain avenue which leads up the valley of the stream always speaks to me of some old-time dwelling which must have stood on the height, for the approach is wide and the beech-trees that line it are very old. The way lies to the right, and soon we are standing on a small plateau carpeted with pine-needles, from which rise one or two tall fir-trees, over-looking the fanlike Falls of Kelty. To-day the solitude is secure. It is good to be alive. Sticks are gathered. One match lights the resinous pine fire. A long column of woodland incense rises into the quiet air. The frugal feast is spread. The peace pipe is lit with that most fragrant of all lighters, a blazing pine faggot. Here is Travellers' Joy complete.

Then, when the daylight fades, and we take the dim path through the twilight woods, what is that round white will-o'-the-wisp which glides so fairy-like between the eerie pines? It is the most mysterious emblem of spring that you will find in the forest. Well might it scare a timid traveller through the dusky woods who did not know something of the wild life of the world. For it is the oriflamme of a young hind or female deer—white, seductive, wonderful—nature's symbol of the flame of love which makes the whole meaning and mystery of the spring.

VII

THE HEART OF THE HIGHLANDS

IN PRAISE OF PETROL

APRIL is the month of surprises. A traveller into the wilds never knows what his luck will be when he puts his hand into nature's weather-bag for a draw. But if we often get the bitters of winter when we expect the balmy blessings of spring, there are other glad surprises of good luck which make us snap our fingers at this dour Scots climate and turn our backs on the east wind. I was just in the act of throwing the old sack over the shoulder for a long trudge south to the Mull of Kintyre when a sudden request came from a friend to take a seat by his driving wheel and act as guide on a little trip into the heart of the Highlands, where he had never been. So I turned north in company instead of going south alone, and the only grudge I now bear against the man at the wheel is, that during a two or three days' run over as many hundreds of miles he saw for the first time, with the help of a little petrol, what took me half a lifetime's leg-work to ferret out in sunshine and storm. The time-table of the modern motorist is so upsetting to the ordinary tramp that while the poor pedestrian stands on the dusty highway, fumbling for his watch to look at the time, his friend has already flown past him and is paying his lunch bill at the next hotel. And yet, from the

standpoint of a man who will leg it slowly into the light
of the last sunset, I will pay this tribute to petrol—the
spirit of the age—that the new generation will see a
thousand miles of their wonderful land for our hundred,
although the balance will always remain with us in
healthy hunger, whipcord muscles, and a knowledge of
the roadside philosophies of common humanity.

We set out one morning when the east winds of
Auld Reekie were flying at our throats, but turning our
backs on them, we made straight for the key to the
North—Stirling. The thirty-six miles between Edinburgh and Stirling were eliminated as soon as possible,
with a thankful look across to Bannockburn, because
the latest historical theory of the battle facts still leaves
the victory with the Scots. Wallace on the Abbey
Craig yonder, and Bruce at Bannockburn—what Scot
ever passes between them on his way to the North
without feeling the whole history of his country welling
up within him! Instead of taking the usual road
through Bridge of Allan and Dunblane, we sweep out
on the long, straight level road for Doune, across the
plain past Ochtertyre and Blair Drummond. Ochtertyre calls to mind John Ramsay, and Blair Drummond
will for ever be associated with Henry Home (Lord
Kames)—both remarkable men in eighteenth-century
Scotland—who are remembered in this district for the
reclamation of what was then called Flanders Moss,
and the establishment of one of the first labour colonies
in this country. For in 1766 Lord Kames resolved to
turn the peat moss of Blair Drummond into fertile
carse land. He floated off the peat into the Forth by
means of little sectional canals. The moss was then
let out to small tenant farmers, who built their homesteads alongside these channels, and were called moss

lairds, forty-two being settled on the land by 1782. The water supply was increased by the erection of a great wheel on the Teith over yonder at Torr Mill. By 1817 there had been reclaimed 1130 acres. An old story, with a wise inference for the agricultural boards to-day. But the sight of Doune Castle, with its dungeons and its machicolations—those murderous holes through which the besieged poured molten lead upon the unlucky heads of the besiegers—makes us forget reclamation schemes, and sing above the hum of the engine the " Bonny Earl of Moray " :—

> " But lang will his ladye
>   Look frae the Castle Doune,
> Ere she see the Earl o' Moray
>   Come soundin' through the toun."

At Kilmahog, a mile beyond Callander, we turned to the left, and made an eight-mile divergence to the Trossachs. Breakfast in Edinburgh and lunch opposite Ellen's Isle, on Loch Katrine, with all the beauties of the April day making this morsel of Highland scenery glow with a thousand reflected wonders in the still waters, and a vision of Scott limping along the shores with his miraculous brain and eyes and ears taking in all the details of the scenery, which he was to make for ever classic to the world in the " Lady of the Lake." Blessed be petrol, which can whisk us so suddenly from all the teasing noises of a town into this fairy solitude, with the blue smoke of the fire rising from the heather knoll into the still air. The workmen are busy at the new road which is to raise the level of Loch Katrine for the third time. How time passes ! Once we pulled our little canoe up the beautiful shingle of the Silver Strand, or all that was left of it. Now you

DOUNE CASTLE

can stand on the new road, and looking over the parapet, see the two older road-levels down in the dim brown waters of Glasgow's big drinking-cup. Once we pulled a little boat on wheels with a rope over the shoulder all the way from yon wood at the end of Loch Vennachar, through the Pass of Leny to Loch Lubnaig, on a weary, wet day—now, we run back to Kilmahog and through the Leny Pass to Loch Lubnaig and Strathyre as quickly as it took us to trudge a mile or so. This time-table revision bothers me so much that there is no chance to tell a tithe of the legends and lore of Lubnaig and Bruce the Abyssinian traveller, of Balquhidder and Rob Roy, until we have topped the long gradient up Glenogle, with its interesting old roads, and are running down the Dochart to Killin.

The sun was shining on the Falls of Dochart as we got out at the bridge and viewed the famous island, with its old weather-beaten pine-trees in the middle of the foam. How often that scene of wild, turbulent waters has been painted from the rock down there by the arch of the bridge ! How often, too, the old Macnabs carried their dead down this island path to the dark burial-place among the trees, with the winter floods making thunder in their ears, and the wail of the pipes making dool in their souls ! Gone for ever are these old fighting lairds from the lands that once were theirs. Some of them sleep in far-off Canadian graves. Some of them sleep here, with the wild waters of their lost home making a never-ending turmoil about their narrow house of death. Better far that the old, fiery, siccar-souled Macnabs should sleep in this isle of thunders and unrest than in a lown level place of graves, where the silence of the glen symbolises the tranquillity of some lesser souls.

It is like coming home, to pass by Glenlochay up the high road and along the braes of Breadalbane, by Morenish and Lawers, with Loch Tay lying stretched below us in all its lordly grandeur. How reminiscent a landscape can be to those who know and love it well! What days are recalled on the Ben up yonder, in sunshine and rain, in snow and hail, in clear still weather when the view was heavenly, and in hurricanes of wind and mist when the blasts took up all efforts at human speech and threw them like the paper letters of a child's game to the maw of the great god Boreas for sport! Near Fearnan the second fire is lit on the shore for tea. As we draw near to Glen Lyon there are voices on every breeze, soft warm hands in the very sunshine, and gleams of love in the ripple of the waves. Kent faces and kind hearts always make the returning a pleasure and the parting a pain. The salmon are leaping in Peter's Pool. The glories of summer and the purple heather are not yet here, but the larches across the river make a delicate green mist against the dim blue hills, and the bare birches lie on the steep slopes like a breath of purple smoke.

Reluctantly turning our backs on Glen Lyon, we take the way that leads down the pleasant vale of Garth by Fortingal to Keltneyburn, where a sharp turn round the end of Coshieville Inn swings us up the steep road to White Bridge. Surely, on a clear day, there are no finer views to be had in the Highlands than up here on the open moors at the back of Schiehallion, 1200 feet above sea-level. The Lassintulich road is not exactly as smooth as a promenade, but it takes you right through a remote wilderness of humpy moors, with Schiehallion's snows gleaming above you in the clouds. On the island of a little moorland loch by the roadside the sea birds rise in white clouds from their nesting place, with a great calling as we pass, and the white of their plumage is outmatched only by the snows of Schiehallion, which looks down on their sanctuary. A plunge through the woods of Lassintullich and Crossmount, a gleam of wind-swept water in the west, and Kinloch-Rannoch, the limit of the day's run, is reached.

Loch Rannoch is as near the heart of Scotland as any place can be, for it is equidistant from the East Neuk of Fife and the wild cliffs of Ardnamurchan, from Inverness in the north and Glasgow in the south—and there is a heavenly outgait to the west when the sun sets behind the mountains of Glencoe and the Shepherds of Etive. That night there was a sound of lake water in our dreams, and the noisy oyster-catchers wakened us at the skreich of day.

Then began another round of wonders as we encircled the loch by Dall, the Black Wood of Rannoch to Bridge of Gaur, and back by the sunny sands of Camusericht to the tiny metropolis of Kinloch in the heart of the Highlands. But the spirit of the car is restless and evidently inexhaustible, so the guide is asked to set another programme, and it is not difficult in this glorious countryside, whose roads are all like old familiar friends.

Eastward again we fly as far as the Struan road-end. Here the ascent is gradual, and superb is the backward view across Tummel side to Schiehallion. As we were running downhill to Trinafour I ventured to suggest that there was a still more glorious 1450-foot road across the hill to Dalnacardoch on the Garry, with a bad surface, and one or two hairpin bends. It was a test road for the car, and a still more test question for

the man who owned the car, for a hardened tramp and
the owner of a first-class car naturally look at roads
from different standpoints. But the man at the wheel
was willing. So, with a sharp turn round the cottage
at Trinafour, we were on the gravel, and gradually
mounting up and round and over the bad bits beyond
the woods of Auchleeks; then a nasty bend at the
junction of the track to Loch Con, and we were past
the worst. But it was worth it all, to be sailing slowly
over these great heather uplands. Away to the north
lay the wild hills of Atholl and Badenoch, with the
shadowy glens about Gaick Lodge beyond Strathgarry.
On every side were trackless mountains and moors.
The air was like a draught of strong waters. When,
after careful going, we reached the Great North Road
at Dalnacardoch, the run continued down the Garry
by Dalnamein and Clunes, Struan and Blair, Killiecrankie and Pitlochry, where, for the mere convention
of a meal, we stopped. But, if this magic country of
mountain and river and moor moves the heart of an
old lover of its natural beauties, what must it be to the
eye and heart of one who travels its bens and glens for
the first time ?

But the last lap was perhaps the best of all, for the
twenty miles up Tummel side to Rannoch combine
more variety of beauty and scenery than can be found
on any other Highland road. Bonskeid is a perfect
paradise of trees. A great capercailzie sat solemnly on
the branch of a pine. The day before, the first cuckoo
was heard in these woods. Here by the entrance there
is a curious candelabra spruce, with four graceful stems
growing straight up from the parent trunk. A few yards
farther on there is an old tree root growing from the
right bank, for all the world like an elephant lowering

LOCH TAY : MORENISH

its trunk on to the road.   But the glory of Tummel side is the Queen's View.   Standing on a bare bluff of rock not far from the roadside, the whole sweep of river, loch, and valley opens out with its greenlands and moorlands, backed by the splendid cone of Schiehallion, rising with its snow-wreathed head into the April skies.   Some views are overrated.   This one is not.   But no words could describe the beauty of these Highland scenes to those who have not seen them in all the glories of their spring and autumn colouring.

Up and down, the road takes us above the loch until at Bridge of Tummel we are in the region of unspoiled heather banks, myriad birchen-trees, and foaming pools, where the brawling stream falls over great masses of rock.   In a little graveyard near Dunalastair sleep many Robertsons, as in a little round stell of death above Loch Tummel sleep many of the dead Highlanders who must have heard Prince Charlie's pipers skirling defiance to Johnny Cope.   As the evening light touches Schiehallion and the far snow-capped hills of Glencoe, we once more reach the loch in the heart of the Highlands, with a sigh of wonder at the things we have seen on the face of the earth in two short days.   It is a triumph of the spirit over the flesh, and of petrol over a pair of old shoes.

And yet, when the darkness falls and a solitary figure stands under the stars, listening to the lap of wavelets on the shore, and the far call of a hoolet in a wood, there comes to mind these words of " A Song against Speed " :—

> " Where is the poet fired to sing
>   The snail's discreet degrees,
>   A rhapsody of sauntering,
>   A gloria of ease ;

Proclaiming theirs the baser part
   Who consciously forswear
The delicate and gentle art
   Of never getting there ?

   .   .   .   .   .

" The turnpike from the car to fling
   As from a yacht the sea,
Is doubtless as inspiriting
   As aught on land can be ;
I grant the glory, the romance,
   But, look behind the veil—
Suppose that while the motor pants
   You miss the nightingale ! "

—E. V. Lucas.

It matters not how we travel so long as we have the heart to love, the eye to see, and the memory to recall the sunny days that were all the sunnier for the presence of someone whose glamorous companionship made the miles seem too short and the steepest braes like level paths. For this is the oldest lesson of the travelling road—that the golden core of life lies in the heart of a friend, and the only thing that lasts is love.

VIII

GLEN LYON

THE LONGEST GLEN IN SCOTLAND

IF a glen is one of Mother Nature's trenches, which worms itself far-ben among the lonely hills, and drains itself dry by means of a river, then the longest in Scotland is assuredly Glen Lyon. It runs from the Appin of Dull to Ben Dorain, and is well over thirty miles in length. But no man was ever able to describe the fairest face on his first meeting with it. So only he who has known and loved this glen for many years, in the joyous summer sunshine and in the early spring-tide snows, exploring the high tops of its great hills and plunging into many of its secret pools for a thrill of refreshing on long, lonely days of gangrel happiness —only he can tell the wonders of this fairest cul-de-sac in Perthshire, and enlighten the mind of many a traveller-in-a-hurry who whisks up to the mouth of it and whisks off again, without dreaming of the glories which lie far up this *gleann dubh crom nan garbh clach*, or dark crooked glen of the great rocks.

To-day it lies sleeping in the August sunshine. But in winter there are places in its narrow throat where, for months on end, the sunshine never falls. Here you will find all that goes to make a Highland glen so wonderful—great mountains lining its sides and guarding its head and foot, sometimes blue-black, under clouds, then all purple and grey-green, or dimly elusive on the still days; flowers banking its long tortuous road, in swathes of blue and white and yellow, the harebells and wild geraniums, the marguerites and stitchwort, the yellow bedstraw and St John's wort laying the grassy borders in carpets of colour; and streams innumerable, tumbling north and south through the wild defiles into the great salmon river which drains with a splendid impetuosity the whole valley, from Loch Lyon far up among the hills, to where it glides, slow and broad-bosomed, into the Tay at the end of Drummond Hill.

But, most of all, the place is steeped in history from end to end. Old battles of the angry clans, cattle reivings, and creach-liftings; killings and intrigues which shook the land from Auld Reekie to St James' with alarm and indignation; old stones, and kirks, and crosses—surely no glen in Scotland is more wonderfully linked to the past and to the ancient Celtic Church than Glen Lyon! Many a saint and *Gillean-Dhe* laboured for God and had his cell in the glen—and as Iona will for ever belong to Columba, so Glen Lyon will for ever belong to his successor and biographer, Adamnan.

Most people approach the glen from Aberfeldy, and in doing so pass the little village of Dull without being conscious that it is there. And yet, Dull is one of the most important spots in the glen's kirk-lore and scholarship. But the glen proper begins with the open dale of Fortingal. Here is one of the neatest and sweetest villages in Scotland, nestling beneath a green, tree-bearded hill, which is topped by an old fort, and faces the purple sides of Drummond Hill across the fertile haughs by the river. At Fortingal there is plenty to whet the antiquary's appetite—stone circles, cup-marked stones, a Roman camp, with an old pagan altarstone resting on the side of the circular site of the headquarters of Septimus Severus (A.D. 209). The beautifully restored parish kirk (for which we have to thank the late Sir Donald Currie) contains some fine work in native oak and, in a little stone recess behind the pulpit, the ancient Celtic hand-bell which was used at many a sacring service.

In the kirkyard you will find, within railings, the remains of the Fortingal yew-tree, which De Candolle assures us is the oldest authentic specimen of vegetation in Europe! A truly courageous statement, especially when tradition adds that Pontius Pilate slept under it. In a private enclosure will also be found an excellent example of a cup-marked stone, and by the side of the door a very old and typical Celtic boulder font. Years ago there used to be some priceless scraps of Celtic carving lying at the back of the church—but these stones have, mercifully, been put under cover.

Beyond the village, and just before you come to the Roman camp, is Glen Lyon House—one of the most romantic and best-preserved old Highland mansions. Seen from the road beyond a green garth, the great old trees screen its harled face, with an indescribable touch of mystery. Dark trees and dark memories surround Glen Lyon House. It was Campbell of Glen Lyon who set out from Achallader Castle for Glencoe, where he received the hospitality of the Macdonalds in their own house, and then rose up with his men, one mid-night, and murdered them. Was there ever a deed which more damnably denied the inviolable law of Highland hospitality!

And now we enter the narrow entrance to the glen

at the Black Wood. The road affords a splendid view
of the Pass of Lyon, where the river comes tumbling
down a straight narrow gorge, lined with trees and
shut in by the towering hills, which seem to encircle
the whole place within the walls of a prison. Standing
here, the thought comes over a true lover of Scotland's
rarest scenery with a grim pathos, that tens of thousands
of travellers elbow one another to see a little snippet of
scenery called the Trossachs, when all over Scotland
there are scenes like this which beggar the path of the
Trossachs for sheer grandeur.

A few hundred yards farther on is Macgregor's
Leap—a leap across the boiling stream from rock to
rock, which a modern athlete of irresponsible age and
with no family ties might still try with a reasonable
hope of success. The two miles between the Pass of
Lyon and the bend of the Black Wood are the finest in
the glen. We have, however, but passed the dark door
of entrance, to which Fortingal's open dale was the
vestibule. Now, we begin the long, closed-in, historic
journey up the glen.

The Highland history of this glen has been made
by the clash and clang of Campbells, Macgregors, and
Menzies, with Columban priests preaching the gospel
of Christ's own peace to soften life for these fighting
clans. At Chesthill House the glen opens out into a
pleasant place of fertile fields and sheep runs. On the
other side of the water a glimpse is got of the ancient
so-called Roman bridge, with its very picturesque
waterfall, and beyond Balintyre the road takes a sudden
turn round a wooded height, on which stands, hidden
in trees, the ruined castle at Carnban. This was the
stronghold of Red Duncan Campbell of the Hospitality,
who died in 1580. The oblong tower, looped and

vaulted, commands the glen up to Inverar and down to Chesthill. Right across the river stands Dericambus amid a little forest of birch-trees. At the bend of the river, above Carnban, a glorious view of the glen is got from the road—the river sweeping round an island, both river banks and island covered with trees, and the great blue hills encircling the whole, while Craig-an-Eilderg stands like a sentinel in the middle horizon.

But the glen is full of memorials to Celtic saints. Here at Invervar, on the right, there is a little lonely square churchyard in a field, a poor place now, but once the chapel of a saint, with a holy well, or *tiobart*, beneath the choir. At Inverinian, across the river, where a stream cuts steep down the hillside in a ravine of trees, the very name commemorates St Ninian. And when we have passed by Ruskich and Slatich we come to that sacred spot, Craig Dianaidh, the Rock of Safety, where, until about 1480, solemn and judicial meetings were held. On the top of the rock, where the judge sat, you will find the traditional footprint of St Peallaidh, or St Palladius, after whom Aberfeldy took its name. A little way beyond this ancient hill of justice, on the left-hand side of the road, stands the cross of St Adamnan, the patron saint of the whole Glen.

Adamnan was Abbot of the monastery at Iona, and wrote the biography of the most sainted of all his predecessors—St Columba, of beloved memory. The name Adamnan means Little Adam, and the Gaelic form of the word—Adhamhnan—sounds in English like Eonan. So, Adamnan has left his Gaelic name of Eonan all up and down the Glen. The Gaelic old story has it that he was banished from Iona because he gave in to the Roman Church on these two vital

E

matters—the tonsure of the crown instead of the Celtic tonsure from ear to ear, and also the date of Easter. So, he, with eleven other *Gillean Dhe* Evangelists, went on a missionary tour to preach peace to the men of Alban. When they landed on the mainland they walked together until they came to Drumalban, across the wilds of Rannoch Moor. On the Ridge of Alban each chose a river for himself, and followed it. St Fillan chose the Dochart, and St Adamnan, or Eonan, chose the Lyon, which led him down the wild valley that was then called *gleann dubh crom nan garbh clach*. At the place now called Milton Eonan, near the Bridge of Balgie, he set up his cell and built a mill, like a good monk who had been used to mingle his devotions with a practical turn for agriculture.

Standing here to-day by this rude stone on which is incised a simple cross, we remember that, long years after his coming, St Eonan stayed the plague which crept stealthily up the Glen from Fortingal. The people, all panic-stricken, implored him to work a miracle : " Eonan of the ruddy cheeks, rise and stay the plague of thy people—save us from death—let it not come upon us east or west."

So the kindly Saint gathered them on the Rock of Safety and calmed their fears by preaching to them the peace of Christ. In a house only forty yards away lay a child dying of the plague. Eonan segregated the people, separating the sound from the unsound, and sent the Glen folks away up to the shielings among the hills. Then he himself went and tended the sick, and the plague was stayed. Lay your hand on this ancient stone of the cross, which is all that is left, probably, of a still older cross, and while you are thanking God for every medical missionary of ancient or modern

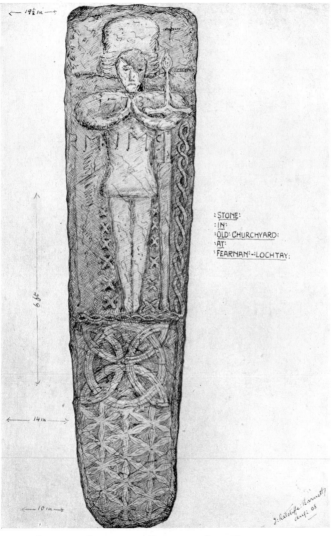

:STONE:
:IN:
:OLD:CHURCHYARD:
:AT:
:FEARNAN:-LOCHTAY:

FEARNAN, LOCHTAY: STONE IN OLD CHURCHYARD

times, who has not been afraid to pass his time among wounded or dying folks—take 127 steps farther up the road, and there, on the right hand-side, among the grass and summer flowers, you will find a rough flat stone lying with a deep hole in it. Here, tradition tells us, Eonan fixed his crucifix when he stayed the plague.

Then as you pass by Camusvrachan, with its one church on this side and its other church on that side of the river—visible monuments of the most famous church case of modern times—look across the river, and away up the valley to the south you will see rising the mighty backs of Ben Lawers and the Stuc. How happy are our memories of a June day long ago up there on the sunlit summit snows, and down in that valley among the ruins of many summer shielings! For, in the springtides of long ago, the young men and maidens drove their herds and flocks to these sweet grazing grounds, while some old men and children and a few matrons kept them company. All the others stayed at home to gather in the harvests. You can see the horses laden with churns and cheese presses, crocks and dairy utensils, pots and crooks, and bags of meal—as this annual flitting to the mountain shielings takes place. Up there old and young are free to wander by the burnsides, among the hills, milking the cows, fishing the streams, and hunting the deer. Many a song was composed and sung by the Highland girls while they milked the cows and thought of their lovers. Did not the tragic incident which served as a foundation for the famous milking song " Colin's Cattle " take place during a cattle raid in this very glen ? And on the summer eves the harp or *clarsach* was brought out to accompany the songs, and round the cottage doors in the gloaming or by the light of the summer moons many a *ceilidh* or story-telling took place. Now the grey-lichened stones and the little recesses for the milking pans in the old ruined walls alone remain to remind us of those happy shieling days.

Across the river yonder the very names of Roro, Roromore, and Roroyere, remind us of the once great family of Macgregor of Roro, to which belonged Sir James Macgregor, Vicar of Fortingal, Notary Public and Dean of Lismore, the first Celt to collect MSS. of Gaelic poetry, whose " Book " lies before us to-day. At Balnahanaid, across the burn from Roromore, there was a relic chapel or " annait," hence the name to-day of *Bal-na-h-annait*, or Place of the Relic Chapel.

But when we cross the Bridge of Balgie we come to St Eonan's real shrine. For here is Milton Eonan, where he had his mill by the stream. A little down the river was his church and cell, which were demolished by Black John of Lorne in 1368. Black John's wife was Janet, a full cousin to King David Bruce, and she complained of the marshy ground about the chapel because she could not go to her devotions without wetting her feet. So Black John built another chapel at *Druim-na-h-eaglais*, now Kerrowmore, but a few hundred yards away, and all that remains of this chapel is the ancient churchyard of Kerrowmore. But, in this churchyard for generations there stood exposed the old Celtic handbell, somewhat similar to, but larger than, the bell in Fortingal Church. This priceless bell of Eonan's Chapel is now in the keeping of the present parish minister at Innerwick. It stands $12\frac{7}{8}$ inches high, is $2\frac{1}{2}$ inches across at its closed-in top, where once was the handle, and $8\frac{3}{8}$ inches at its wide-mouthed bottom. Made of iron and riveted, it has evidently been enamelled or beaten over with bronze, and even to-day its tone is rich and solemn when touched. This is the most precious relic of the Celtic Church in Glen Lyon to-day.

And what of Adamnan's end ? When Little Adam, called Eonan, lay dying, he instructed his people to place his body on a bier, and run *lunnan*, or bearing sticks, through rings of withies (*dullan*). Then they were to carry him down the river until a withy ring or *dul* broke. When the first *dul* broke, there they were to bury him. They did so, and called the place Dull. At Dull they built a church over his grave and raised a school and college—said to be the first seminary of education on the mainland of Scotland. At Dull to-day stands a primitive old cross with one arm broken off. Dull became such a famous educational centre that the King afterwards gave the *Gillean-Dhe* at Dull a city of refuge garth marked by large stones, and also a lord-ship, which to this day is called the Abba-land of Dull, or Appin of Dull. The famous common house and schools were removed from Dull, in the middle centuries, to Dunkeld, and then at a later date to St Andrews, which became the first university in Scotland. Thus Adamnan, or Eonan, will ever be associated with the foundation of our oldest university.

Before leaving Kerrowmore, near the Bridge of Balgie, it is well to note the circular mound, with a flat top, called *Tom-na-Cuartaig* or Hill of the Circle. This is probably the ancient folk-mote, where justice was dispensed ; and near-by are the ruins of the chief's castle—*Tigh Iain Duibh nan lann*—Black John of the Spears' House, the same John of Lorne who was married to King David Bruce's cousin Janet, who was so scrupulous about wet feet on Sundays.

Beyond Bridge of Balgie the Glen extends for many

miles. Here stands Meggernie Castle, a stately, white Highland home, in green fields by the river, and approached by an avenue of fine old beech- and lime-trees. Meggernie Castle was built by *Colin Gorach*, Mad Colin, son of Red Duncan, about 1582. It was enlarged by his great-grandson, the Glen Lyon Campbell of unhappy memories, who carried the curse of Glencoe. After the massacre he was ordered to Flanders with his regiment. He never returned, but died at Bruges on 2nd August 1696, at the age of sixty-five.

> " He smiled as a friend while he planned as a foe,
> To redden each hearthstone in misty Glencoe."

Meggernie then passed to the Atholl Murrays, who greatly improved the roads and worked the lead-mines at Kerrowmore. From them it passed to the Menzies family, and it was Colonel James Menzies of Culdares who planted the great larches behind the gardens at Meggernie, said by tradition to be the first larches introduced to Scotland from Tyrol. But that is another story, which might be questioned at Blair Castle and Monzie Castle.

Beyond Meggernie the road, a rather rough one, leads away up to Invermeran, on Loch Lyon. Up here, by Cashlie (Castles), there are some fine old Fingalian towers, or watch forts. " Fingal had twelve castles in the crooked glen of large stones," as the old Gaelic legend has it, and five of these watch towers can still be traced, each with its Fingalian name. Beyond Loch Lyon lies the waste of Drumalban, with Duncan Ban Macintyre's great hill of Ben Doran guarding the wild scene. Even here, at the very head of the longest glen in Scotland, near Drumalban, there was still another relic chapel or " annait " of some saint.

Ancient days and hoary memories crowd upon us as we sit and play a lament or a battle march in the glen, with a sob in the chanter and a roar in the drones, for every lost love or clan feud of Campbell, Macgregor, or Menzies. They will never come again. Strangers sit by their hearths. But the blood and spirit and Celtic fire remain to-day wherever the old songs are sung or the new challenge to the fight is sounded in the ears of their children's children.

IX

MACGREGOR'S LEAP

A LEGEND OF GLEN LYON

IN the narrow Pass of Lyon there is a wild gorge well known to travellers. Here local history tells us a Macgregor long ago leaped in desperation from one side of the river to the other. To this rock many tourists make their way in summer-time, and having gazed across the heady torrent, they turn away wondering what the story is, and why mortal man was ever so bereft of his senses as to attempt that mad jump. But, although Macgregor's Leap brings many wandering folks to the sublime gateway of the glen, they have no more seen the glen than a man standing on the doorstep can see the hidden treasures of a Duke's castle. The glen, moreover, is steeped in legendry. Here, for centuries, Macgregors and Campbells mingled their hostilities with the reds and greens of their kilts, as to-day the rowan berries splash the dark foliage of the mountain ash with spots of blood. But it is hard to get the truth of any tale from three different clansmen in the one way. This, however, is the tale of Macgregor's Leap as you may get it from one or other of the wise men in the long glen to-day.

Long ago, a Macgregor of Glen Lyon who wished to join his clan at Balquhidder passed up the glen and over the hills to Glen Lochay, near Killin. He knew that he was in the country of his enemies, the Campbells, but he was both tired and hungry, and a hungry man is a risky man. So, he ventured to draw near a cottage, and began to reconnoitre his chances. Just then a girl came out and slowly went down to the stream for water—an innocent-looking Campbell girl, who gave no sign that her father and brother had sent her on this bogus errand as a decoy. Suddenly she lifted her eyes and saw the hungry Macgregor. Womanlike, she invited him to come in and have a refreshment. Manlike, despite his scruples, he followed her. But, before entering, he looked round suspiciously, as a Macgregor in his circumstances might well do.

" Do you not trust me, just man ? " she said to him in a hurt voice.

" Have you never heard," replied the hungry man, " that the stag sniffs the air of the pool before he drinks ? "

And with that they entered the cottage. Once inside, she gave him a cogie of milk to drink. Feeling himself now safe behind the courtesies of Highland hospitality, he raised the cogie to drink, when she dashed the milk into his eyes. In a trice her father and brother sprang on him from behind. But the Macgregor, drawing his sword, cut backwards—killed the one—dirked the other—and was flying for the hill before a Campbell had time to draw breath or whistle an alarm. Up and up he climbed until he reached the top, then doubled back again down Glen Lochay. Peering cautiously through birk and bracken, he saw Campbell of Lochay and his men emerging from Lochay House with four bloodhounds to track him down. He could even hear the dogs baying in the valley far below.

So the Macgregor made his way down the glen until he reached Loch Tay. He waded into the water up to the neck, and slowly but surely, sometimes wading, sometimes swimming, travelled down the shore to Lawers—a long and desperate journey in the chilly loch. At Lawers, being utterly exhausted, he knocked at the door of Campbell of Lawers, the ruins of whose house you may still see on the shore to-day.

"Shelter, and protection—is it here ?—for a hard-pressed man—and food ?" gasped the Macgregor.

"Yes — come in," said Campbell of Lawers. And immediately the fugitive was hidden in the barn.

Campbell of Lochay, having tracked his prey to the head of the loch by means of the bloodhounds, lost the trail where the Macgregor had entered the water. So he sent two dogs round the other side of Loch Tay, and took two with him down the Lawers side. At Lawers they picked up the scent again, and Campbell of Lochay was soon knocking at the door of the Laird of Lawers. He demanded that the Macgregor should be given up to him, for he knew he was there. Lawers, being a Highland gentleman, remembered the obligations of hospitality once given, and made answer accordingly.

"Yes—he is safely behind my doors. But, before claiming him, come in and eat with me."

So they dined and they drank. But, while they were eating and drinking in the hall, Macgregor got the hint, and climbed through the thatch of the barn roof while his enemies lay outside the door. Racing down the lochside to Fearnan, he crossed by Auchtar and Croftgarrow, into Glen Lyon. But the dogs were already after him, hot-scented, and the two hounds from Lawers had now been joined by the other two that had circled the loch. The pace was terrific as they turned into the Pass of Lyon. Nothing could save the Macgregor now. Except a leap across the river ! It was death either way. And yet there was one mad chance left in the leap. So, with the breath of the first bloodhound on him, he ran down the rocks and leaped across the boiling river, where it still roars between the rocks. Bruised and bleeding, he just managed to scramble up the farther rock. The first dog leaped after him, and fell short into the boiling stream of death. The second did the same. The third, taking a mightier stride, reached the rock on which the bleeding Macgregor crouched waiting. One stroke of the dirk sent it after the other two, to be drowned in the flood of Lyon. The fourth dog was in the act of springing after its three companions, when Campbell, not wishing to lose his last dog, caught it by the tail and drew it back.

Then up and off the Macgregor ran again, threading his way stealthily by Dericambus and Inverinian. Somewhere near Ruskich or Slatich he forded the river. On the north bank he met a shepherd, and told him that the Black Dog of the Campbells was after him.

"Run on, friend," said the shepherd, "and fear nothing."

And the weary Macgregor ran on.

The shepherd folded his arms across his breast and slowly walked down the Glen. At the corner where the road winds round the Rock of Justice, on the top of which is imprinted the footstep of St Palladius, and not a great way from the Cross of St Adamnan, the man of sheep met the only remaining Black Dog, loping sullenly round the rock ahead of the following Campbells. Without unfolding his arms, the shepherd kicked the dog with terrific force under the jaw, and it fell dead. There, just within the wooden paling, you can still see the Clach-na-Cuin—the Stone of the Dog —as it has been called from time immemorial. The Campbells came up peching with anger, and accused the shepherd of slaughter. But, on solemn oath, he threeped that he had neither unfolded his arms nor laid a finger on the dog.

So the Macgregor continued his flight, travelling now from tree-top to tree-top, until he reached Inner-wick, where the old hill road crosses north to Rannoch— a most glamorous hill track still. In the Black Wood of Dall, on Loch Rannoch side, he lived in exile for years among those great trees whose roots and branches were there before history began.

But, the heart always calls us home, and the out-lawed Macgregor grew tired of his exile at the long last. So he went secretly to the Laird of Chesthill, in Glen Lyon, and begged him to intercede with Campbell of Lochay for his pardon. Chesthill, knowing the brave man's story, agreed. " But," said he, " you must take the message to Lochay yourself. Are you willing to do this daring thing ? "

The home hunger burned in the Macgregor's heart.

" Yes—I will do it."

So Chesthill gave him a letter, and the Macgregor took it himself to the very door of Campbell of Lochay. It contained these words—" Grant pardon to a man who is brave enough to go to the door of his enemy and ask for it himself."

The pardon was granted, and the Macgregor

returned to the glen of his heart. He spent his last years as a very old man in the little farm of Tynayere, close by the salmon pool of Lyon, which fishers now call Peter's Pool. It is within a mile or so of the famous gorge, which to the end of time will bear his name—Macgregor's Leap.

X

THE OLDEST WEAPON IN THE WORLD

AN ARCHER'S REVERIE

VERIFYING a tradition with a six-foot bow and a twenty-eight-inch arrow is a heartsome game for an archer-antiquary, especially when the scene of action is the longest glen in Scotland, and the place of testing is an old ruined castle on a height above a river—remote, silent, and hill-encircled, sleeping in the late September sun. The native historian of the glen at Woodend may well be pardoned for having mistaken the bow, in its waterproof case, for a fishing-rod, for it is more than probable that no one has shot an arrow from Red Duncan's castle for hundreds of years. The glen, however, is full of tradition about ancient bowmen, and in these modern days, when archery is almost extinct, it was like bridging the centuries to hear the twang of the string on the castle ramparts. Glen Lyon has at least three well-known traditions of Highland archers.

In the time of Black John of the Spears (1350), a Chisholm made a raid on the glen. John of Lorne had only his seven sons at home to act as a bodyguard, four on the right and three on the left, in his castle near Bridge of Balgie, so, to make up the odd number and equalise the flanks, he called in a very manly fellow, a cobbler, whose name was M'Callum. The

GLEN LYON : BRIDGE OF BALGIE

day was sultry, and the Chisholm, who doubtless knew that most of the Campbells were away on some reiving ploy of their own, rode carelessly up the riverside in his heavy armour at the head of his men. In the great heat he raised the visor of his helmet for a moment to wipe the sweat from his brow. M'Callum the Cobbler —*Greusaiche Riabhach*—saw the movement from the castle, nocked an arrow, raised his bow, loosed the shaft, and the Chisholm fell from his horse, with the arrow pinning his right hand to his brow. A namely shot and no mistake.

Farther down the glen you can see the old archery butts at Tulloch Callum or Callum's Mound. Here, where a few trees now stand, the bowmen gathered to shoot their arrows at a mark on yon green hillock across the water by Roroyere. It is a very long shot, about 350 yards by the ordnance map, and one naturally wonders if the tradition is true.

Still farther down the glen stands the Castle of Carnban, the home of Red Duncan of the Hospitality, who died in 1580. As his name indicates, he was a generous-hearted man and kept open door to the strolling minstrels of that day. But soon after his death a company of Lochaber men swept down on the glen. The castle stands splendidly on a high spit of land overlooking the river and must have been hard to take. So, tradition tells us that the robbers took their stand on the other side of the river, sheltered doubtless by some trees for fear of the castle arrows, and one of the Lochaber gentry shot a well-aimed arrow with a piece of burning lint attached right into the roof of the castle. The dry thatch took fire and Carnban was burned to the ground, never to be built again. There the ruin stands to-day on its height above the road,

smothered in trees which are of comparatively modern
growth. From the nearest clear space on the same
height, but farther away from the river, I took my
stand, nocked two old arrows, and shot them towards
the river. One struck in a bit of turf among the stones
of the river bed, the other stood a few yards from the
first among the brushwood—not quite 200 yards in all.
As I used only a 44-lb. self-lancewood bow which is
now inclined to follow the string, and the distance was
farther from the river than the castle itself, it is certain
that Red Duncan's castle was easily reached by an
arrow with a flaming lint attached, if shot by a skilled
archer who used a strong bow. Thus may an ancient
tradition be verified, and the truth of it established
after a lapse of three hundred years.

Many fabulous tales, of course, are told of the long-
distance shooting of these ancient archers, and we are
apt to doubt them unless we have accurate knowledge.
Shakespeare tells us in the Second Part of " Henry IV."
about old Double, who " *clapped i the clout at twelve
score ; and carried yon aforehand shaft a fourteen and
fourteen-and-a-half, that it would have done a man's
heart good to see.*"

So to hit the clout in Shakespeare's time at 240 yards
was a great feat, and to shoot a flight arrow 280 or
290 yards was good shooting. But the greatest English
archer of modern times, Mr Horace Ford, shot 308 yards
in 1856 with a 68-lb. bow. That was considered at
the time a great record for an English bow, and Mr Ford
himself said that it might safely be asserted that few
archers could cover a distance of 300 yards.

But in this, as in all other kinds of sport, records
are being continually broken, and the Turkish bow
has outdistanced anything that was ever done by the

English bow.   I have before me a letter from Mr Ingo Simon, a member of the Royal Toxophilite Society, in which he says : " I shot in 1914 at La Toquet 462 yards and some inches.   I feel sure that if I had not had my good bows and arrows stolen, I should have attained a distance of 500 yards sooner or later.   Mahmoud Effendi shot, as you probably know, 482 yards before members of the Tox in 1792, or about then—Sir Ralph Payne Gallwey had a very detailed account, written by Sir Thomas Frankland, who was an eye-witness of this. This must be in possession of Sir John Payne Gallwey now.   The record distance, marked on the old Maidan near Constantinople, is 810 yards.   I can quite believe this—a whole nation trained to archery might well produce the strength and skill combined, plus the tradition and perfect tackle.   The arrow, of course, is just as important as the bow.   I have in my possession a Turkish bow that is so strong that I cannot draw it more than about twenty inches ; also a Persian one, which is about as strong.   Now a man that could use such a bow easily would do some long shooting.   There is no question that the Turkish bow is by a good long way the most perfect bow that has ever been made. It is like the modern high-velocity rifle as compared to large bores and black powder."

Of course, Mr Ingo Simon was using a Turkish bow and arrows when he made his record.   So far as I know, it has never been beaten by another British bowman.   But it all goes to prove that our forefathers may have done far greater things with the bow than we can even imagine now.

To-day, alas, archery is a dying sport in our land. Hundreds of years ago it was a compulsory practice in Scotland.   James I. was a great encourager of archery.

F

All persons over twelve years of age were ordered to be archers, bowmarks were set up near every parish church, and all boys over thirteen and men who did not practise archery were fined. James II. was even more severe, for football and golf were in those ancient days very popular games, but the King decreed that football and golf were to be " utterly cried down, and not to be used." James III. and James IV. made similar laws enforcing archery. Parliament insisted on it even after the reign of James V. Queen Mary, we know, was a skilled archer, having butts both at Holyrood and at St Andrews. Only two days after the murder of Darnley, her husband, she arrived on Sunday at Seton Castle with Bothwell, and immediately consoled her widow's heart with a contest at archery. She and Bothwell won the match against Seton and Huntly, and the losers entertained the winners to a dinner in a tavern at Tranent.

The West of Scotland was especially the home of archery, and for generations Kilwinning and Irvine were centres of the papingo. Even thirty-five years ago, in an old Renfrewshire town, there was a shop, just across the river, and within sight of the ancient Abbey of St Mirren, which did a regular trade in the sale of good bows. There my first bow was bought. But to-day the sport of Toxophilus is almost dead, and the Royal Company of Archers in Edinburgh are the last real representatives of the oldest soldiers in the world — those Stone Age warriors who lived in caves and tipped their primitive arrows with rough flint heads.

Tradition, however, is often a lying jade. We have an instance of this within the new Edinburgh city boundary. Near the gate of Cramond Kirk there is a

Loch Oich near Aberchalder and Invergarry

tree with a thin iron shaft stuck in one of the high branches. In light of the undoubted fact that in the time of James I. the shooting butt was always near the parish church, it was natural that I should listen with solemn interest one day to the statement of an old inhabitant who showed me the shaft. He told me that it was an ancient arrow shaft, and added something about Cramond being an old Roman station. Knowing, however, that arrows were never wholly made of iron shafts, and remembering Jonathan Oldbuck and his ultra-enthusiasm in spotting antiquities, I pursued my inquiries further. A second resident informed me that the iron shaft in the tree was a ramrod which some early Victorian Volunteer, in his nervous enthusiasm, had shot by mistake out of his antique rifle when practising the defence of his country. Still a third native of Cramond, who is of older standing than the other two, assured me with a smile that the rod is just an old partan hook for catching crabs !

The flight of an arrow is a perfect poem of motion. To stand in some wide green pleasaunce and draw an arrow to the pile until the right hand just touches the chin, and send the delicate shaft up into the blue with a clean loose and a twang of the string, watching it climb the sky to the summit of its flight, then a little pause as it turns in the sun and swiftly descends, a thing of life and beauty, to bury its steel point in the emerald turf two hundred yards away—this is to feel the archer's happy thrill.

To a perfervid Scot, one of the most moving sights in Edinburgh is the Flodden Bow in the Archers' Hall— a simple knotted weapon of yew, which was preserved for centuries in a house near Flodden Field. To a Scot who is blessed with a historic memory, there is always a sound of keening in history, and the sight of this old bow brings the twist of pain to our hearts. For Flodden is our national wailing-place, our field of lost chances and slain hopes, where the flower of Scots chivalry made a cordon of dead nobles and gentlemen around their fallen King. There the English arrows fell thick on them as flakes of snow. There some one twanged the string of this very ancient bow, and sent a swift and silent death-pang through some Scotsman's heart with a flight of each arrow. What tales of splendid bravery might not this old bow tell! Four hundred years of clash and clang since Flodden to the great World War—yet the " Flowers of the Forest " is our ageless coronach of death!

The last time bows were used in a Scots battle was at Tippermuir in 1644, when Lord Kilpont commanded the bowmen, who were on the left of Montrose's army. There is, it is true, a tradition that bows were used as late as 1688 at a great clan battle between the Mackintoshes and the Macdonalds, but this is very doubtful. It is, however, incontestably true that Sir James Turner wrote in 1670 : " The bow is now in Europe useless." And the very last offensive use of the bow in Scotland took place in 1791, when two gentlemen fought a duel in Edinburgh with bows and arrows, shooting three arrows each. By the mercy of Heaven, and their own utter lack of skill, no damage whatever was done.

The Royal Company of Archers and King's Body-guard, whom all Edinburgh schoolboys have seen shooting in the Meadows, have annals which date back to 1676. This is the oldest archers' company in Britain. Some indeed have ventured the opinion that the Royal Company was a survival of the old Scots

Guard of France, which consisted of 100 *gens d'armes* and 200 archers. The Scots Guard originated among those Scots who survived the Battle of Verneuil (1424) and did not wish to return home. The first captain of this namely guard was John Stewart, Lord of Aubigné, who founded a great Scots house in France. But the connection between the Royal Company of Archers and the old Scots Guard of France is mere conjecture. In the year 1703, however, a charter of incorporation was granted to the Royal Company by Queen Anne, the *reddendo* or service to be performed being the presentation of a pair of barbed arrows if required. To this day, when the King comes to Edinburgh, and the Bodyguard of Archers is on duty, the *reddendo* of arrows is presented.

All lovers of the bow delight to honour the memory of Roger Ascham, the quaint sixteenth-century writer of *Toxophilus, or the Schole of Shootinge*. Ascham was born only two years after the Battle of Flodden. His book, once a living text-book of English archery, is still unsurpassed as a guide to the use of the long bow ; but, alas ! to-day our children know it only as an ancient classic of English literature, and learn its immortal sentence on the five points of archery as a mere task of memory : " *Standynge, nockyng, drawyng, holdyng, lowsing, whereby cometh fayre shotynge.*" It is the final proof of the passing of the long bow, which in this country is now only used by a few enthusiastic toxophilites. But still, when we handle a flint arrowhead or look with reverence on the Flodden Bow ; when we stand on Red Duncan's castle verifying tradition, or send an arrow into the red or gold of the great targets on a summer evening ; we hear across the centuries this Savage Song of the Bow, which Eurytus sang in Homeric times, and we know that we are handling the oldest weapon in the world :—

> " Keen and low
>   Doth the arrow sing,
> The Song of the Bow,
>   The sound of the string,
> The shafts cry shrill :
>   Let us forth again,
> Let us feed our fill
>   On the flesh of men."

—ANDREW LANG.

XI

THE VOYAGE OF THE "KELPIE"

A CANOEING CRUISE IN SCOTLAND

THE true principle of sport may be summed up in the words "Do it yourself." Whenever we begin to hire other people, the strenuousness, the initiative, the pleasure, and the knowledge become second-hand, and the whole adventure of brain, health, and even muscle suffers. This applies to stalking a stag, landing a fish, sailing a boat, or walking the world. As a wise modern essayist puts it—I have two doctors; the first is my right leg, the second is my left. That is the quintessence of the spirit of sport. You cannot buy it. There is only one way to learn it. Do it yourself.

It was a long time ago, and canoeing has gone out of fashion since them. But I have just been over the old ground, the old waters, the old haunts—and I have found only one grey-haired Highlander at Inversnaid who remembers the *Kelpie* and her owners.

To begin with, we built her ourselves in the old coachhouse at home, where there never was a coach in our time. The skipper calculated her weight to a pound when he drew the plans, and the cook smiled incredulous. But when the long, shapely, wooden, flat-bottomed canoe was finished, with her centre-board, her two masts and sails, her water-tight compartments and lockers all varnished to a glossy mahogany in which you could see your face well enough to shave, we took her to the great scales at the mill, and she turned them only four pounds over the calculated weight. I can understand it now, for the skipper was afterwards to design and build floating palaces for millionaires and to stand before kings—whereas the cook only did what he was told, hammering nails and doing the drudgery of a common carpenter or orraman. However, at long last, in the early days of June (1890) the *Kelpie* was finished and photographed. A pair of light wheels with an adjustable axle, which could be stowed away forward; two snow-white lug-sails, a couple of white sailor bags with a change of clothing, one in the forward hatch, the other in the after hatch; a little blue silk Scots flag with a white St Andrew's Cross sewed by the dear old lady, and we were completely furnished for an inland voyage through Scotland's lochs, rivers, and roads.

When we set off for a two weeks' cruise the *Kelpie* had never even been in the water. We lived two miles from the launching place. But our faith in her was not misplaced, and she fulfilled all our expectations on river, road, or sea. It was four o'clock one fine June morning when we trundled her on the axle and wheels out of the front gate, and along the road for some miles, to a spot near Linwood, on the River Cart in Renfrewshire. No champagne bottle was broken at that launch, for we simply grasped our paddles and stepped in. Then, slowly we caught the current, and avoiding a snag here and there we passed down the Cart by Renfrew, and came into the Clyde when the great shipyards were waking up the new day with the noise of a thousand rivets and hammers. A tiny little ship of fourteen feet with two men sitting face-forward in a square well, mutually dependent on every movement of body, with an instinctive knowledge of ropes and paddles and sails, for a whole fortnight, in rain and shine, squall or calm—that was our daily world. With the right men there was no danger—with the wrong men death from drowning or misery from incompatibility was an hourly possibility. Thus do two men in one canoe make a complete test of disposition, nerve, and common sense.

Our first adventure began as we rounded Dumbarton Rock to ascend the River Leven. For the Leven is a tidal river, and we were half an hour late for the tide ! So we paddled bravely up to the town with bare arms, and muscles strained like whipcords, until we saw that the river had already begun to race below the bridge, on which were standing hundreds of workmen from the yards. It was a toss-up whether we could beat the current—but we were both gymnasts—so foot by foot we held our own, until we passed triumphantly below the bridge to the cheers of the crowd on the parapet. The general public may not know that the Vale of Leven is famous for Turkey red calico works. The cook found that out as he was walking up stream with the towing rope over his shoulder, literally wading through the thickly-dyed water which was polluted by the overflow from the mills. But by the mercy of Heaven, a horse was towing a launch up the river to Balloch, on Loch Lomond, and the owner very kindly threw us a line. Once the rope broke. But soon our troubles were over, and we were floating on the limpid waters of that queen of lochs where we were to spend days of idyllic pleasure with paddle and sail.

Balloch, Luss, Inverbeg, Tarbet, Inversnaid—we stayed at all these pleasant hostelries. We visited all the islands, paddling when there was no wind, hoisting our sails when the breeze was favourable, centre-board down, and sitting on the windward combing of the well as the *Kelpie* raced along under double lug-sails, like a white-winged spirit.

Happy memories crowd upon one another still. The cook carried a banjo, on which he serenaded many an astonished damsel, like the maid of Inchmurren, the girl at Luss, the ladies on the road near Inverbeg. Ah me! They must all be old women now. For is not the cook himself turning grey? But there was a real tone of pathos (or was it laughter?) in his voice as he sat forlorn on the roadside in the rain and sang "Home, Sweet Home!" while the skipper turned his face to the trees until the ladies were past. One sight lingers with me still—it was the island of Inchcailleach near Balmaha, seen from its highest point on a perfect June day, with its woodland glades one mass of blue hyacinths, reminding one of Tennyson's beautiful figure in *Guinevere*—

> "sheets of hyacinths
> That seemed the heavens upbreaking thro'
> The earth."

But it was not always sunshine. There were days of storm, when we were unable to launch the *Kelpie*. There is a spot above Tarbet where dinner had to be cooked in a pine wood amid torrents of rain. The rain got into the soup, the bread was sopping wet, and the greasy tin dishes had to be washed in cold water with Monkey Brand. But our hearts were warm as we paddled in oilskins all the way to Inversnaid through sheets of rain.

The road from Inversnaid to Loch Katrine begins with a very steep hill behind the hotel, and for this

steep brae we hired a cart. At the top of the hill the
Kelpie was set on her own wheels, and we set off on
our five or six miles' trundle across the hills. Midway
across the moors we halted for a rest near Loch Arklet.
The cook sat on the canoe amidships, twanging his
guitar and singing—

> " The beautiful isles of Greece,
>   Full many a bard has sung,
> But the isles I love best lie far in the west,
>   Where men speak the Gaelic tongue.
> Jerusalem, Athens, and Rome,
>   I would see them before I die ;
> But I'd rather not see any one of the three
>   Than be banished for ever from Skye."
>   —SHERIFF NICOLSON.

A shooting party came over the heather, crossed the
road, stared open-eyed at the sight of a boat high up
among the hills, and listened to the song with a smile.
Later on we were to meet the shooters in very different
circumstances.

Launching our craft again at Stronachlachar, we
sailed and paddled down Loch Katrine in the sunset.
We had a delicious supper by a burn on the lochside,
with new-laid eggs which were bought at a little farm.
While we cooked the eggs and sat at our evening meal
the farmer's wife came to the door again and again,
and shading her eyes in the sunset light, looked down
the road. She told us that she was expecting her old
mother. At last a cart came rumbling along the shore
with a country kist in it, and on the top of the kist sat
a sweet old woman in a mutch, with the young farmer
walking by her side. The resplendent light of evening
was all aglow on her expectant face. It was exactly at
this part of the road that Wordsworth long ago met a

country traveller in just such a sunset hour, and was greeted by the ever memorable words which became the subject of one of his poems :—

"What ! are you stepping westward ? "

The meeting of the old mother and her daughter at the farm door was a holy thing to see, and added a touch of mystical wonder to the radiant sunset. The memory of that lambent poem, after a lapse of fifty years, moves us still.

While paddling down the loch after our simple supper, a large steam launch called the *Goblin* passed us, with the shooting party on board, and field-glasses were turned on the tiny canoe. The only place likely for us to stay the night was a gamekeeper's cottage, of which we had been told, so we made for the beach at Brenachoile Lodge. No sooner had we landed than the skipper of the *Goblin* came along and handed us a letter addressed " To the Gentlemen in the Canoe." It was a kind invitation to spend the evening at the lodge. So having made our toilets at the gamekeeper's, we were soon ushered into the lodge living-room— a large octagonal apartment full of Eastern rugs, and lamps and hangings. A very old gentleman in a velvet coat lay on a sofa. His son—a striking-looking man with a long black beard, was dressed in blue evening jacket and trousers, with a blue silk cummerbund round his waist. There were several others—men and women—in the house party, and the talk was soon of boats and sport, South African rivers, and Indian canoes. Kindness, like a heavenly memory, stays with us all our lives. But alas ! on a sunny Sunday, but a few weeks ago, I saw the wreck of the old *Goblin*. I attended worship in the beautiful little parish church at the Trossachs, and there I saw memorials to all the friends of that evening at Brenachoile. The east window is in remembrance of the old gentleman ; the memorial outside is for his black-bearded son ; the newly-erected brass is in memory of the two brave lads, his only sons, who were killed in the Great War. Three generations completely wiped out, and none now to carry on the name of those who loved their lands from Glenbruach to Inversnaid. *Sic transit gloria mundi.*

The glow-worms in the wood at Brenachoile had all their lamps lit that night. But next morning it made our Scots hearts laugh to be charged 16s. for a bite of breakfast and the privilege of sleeping on the floor of a gamekeeper's cottage. We paddled slowly past the beautiful silver strand (now completely submerged), and landed on Ellen's Isle. The cook, in his romantic search for the ghostly maid, found a yellow rose lying crushed and faded. On a summer day the Trossachs end of Loch Katrine is a very lovely bit of Highland scenery.

A trundle on wheels brought us to Loch Achray, down which we raced with the lug-sails drawing famously. Between Loch Achray and Loch Vennachar the river was navigable, but gave us some exciting moments. Boots and stockings off, the cook sat stride-legs across the bow with a paddle in his hand—the skipper sat likewise across the stern—and between careful paddling and a good deal of foot work against dangerous rocks, the rapids were shot, and Loch Vennachar was reached in safety. At the eastern end of this loch we cooked a big supper in a fir wood, secured the *Kelpie*, hid some luggage up a tree, and trudged in the dark to Callander for a bed. Next morning, when we walked back, the canoe was easily found, but we could not locate the tree. After an anxious search, we found it, and breathed freely again. Then the rain came down in torrents, and for five weary miles we hauled our craft through the Pass of Leny to Loch Lubnaig, almost parboiled in oilskin coats, trousers, and sou'-westers. An afternoon sail in clear weather up Loch Lubnaig brought us to Strathyre, where we rested pleasantly over a never-to-be-forgotten week-end, being the first visitors at a newly-opened hotel.

But, having brought a boat into the heart of Scotland, the problem was how to get it out again. So we ordered a carriage truck from Oban, shipped the *Kelpie* on the train, and disembarked her at Stirling Station. Next morning we began the long, tortuous journey down the Links of Forth. The wind and tide were with us, and we raced full sail down the river with a strong breeze and a fiery sun burning our bare arms. That was long before the great docks at Grangemouth were made, and in the furious race down-stream between high mud-banks we were blown past the old entrance to Grangemouth Canal at the Carron River. Sail was lowered, and soon we were paddling right across the wide estuary towards a distant town of smoke and chimneys. All of a sudden in the midst of the angry waste of seas the *Kelpie* was nearly wrecked on a hidden sandbank a mile or two from land. But we shoved off into deep water again, and made for the unknown town. It was Bo'ness—where twenty years after, strange to say, the cook was to make his home for eight years. I can remember the old harbour, the vennel, the quaint tavern at the quayhead where we had a ham-and-egg tea. At the turn of the tide we

THE KELPIE, 1890

BUILT BY JAMES RENNIE BARNETT AND THOMAS RATCLIFFE BARNETT

paddled back to Grangemouth. Hundreds of people crowded round us as we landed at the old canal basin. Next day we began the long journey through the Forth and Clyde Canal, working every lock, spending one night at Kilsyth, and another at Kirkintilloch—with creepy memories of an inn in Kilsyth. It was a Friday afternoon when we reached Bowling on the Clyde. After a good night's sleep at home, we returned next day and trundled the *Kelpie* ten miles over Renfrewshire roads to a little loch near Bridge of Weir—having covered over two hundred miles by land and water in a fortnight.

Would that it all might come again! It meant a lot of work before setting out. It meant hard exercise and perfect health while we were on the cruise. But it left us with undying memories of a thousand and one adventures, of idyllic days and nights, and of a land glamorous with history and beauty which draws the heart of a Scot with a love that is better than life.

XII

AN OLD HIGHLAND HOUSE

AND ITS ROMANTIC STORY

IT was in the old Highland house that I first heard this brave Stewart toast—" My King, my King! Oh for three hands—two for the pipes and one for the claymore ! "

That ancient Royal pledge gives the whole atmosphere of the stories which sough through the haunted rooms and the armour-studded hall like the moaning of wintry winds. For kings and chieftains, from the six Jameses to Tearlach Og, from the phantom Major with his speckled gun to the faithful Jacobite John who stood by the hapless Prince to the last day of life—they all go to make up the tale of this ancient Highland house.

It stands to-day, looking up to the great Ben, with windows that twinkle like an old man's eyes in the morning sun. Small-turreted at the corners, the conglomeration of many buildings of different dates, neither too large nor too small, surrounded by immemorial trees and lawns, from which you can see the gleam of the loch and hear the perpetual cry of whaups or the gluck of little waves, this ivy-covered dwelling by the lochside is an aggregate of Highland history writ deep in the blood of the dead gallants whose claymores and targes hang eloquent in the hall to-day.

Royal by name and race, this sept of the Stewarts goes far back to the dims of Scots history, when a Stewart, the Duke of Albany, was Governor of Scotland from 1420 to 1424. But a plague on dates! Holding land by charter from the middle of the fifteenth century, the first Stewart of this sept settled on this spit of land on the lochside below the great Ben in the year 1586, and his death-stone can be seen to this day in the old ruined kirk of Dundurn.

But, like all his race in those old fighting days, he went down in blood, being murdered by the Macgregors. He, too, knew the road to the Glen of Weeping, for, along with his cousins of Appin, he had a hand in a cruel tulzie with the M'Ians of Glencoe—a bill that was to be paid for dearly in the next generation, as we shall see.

To-day the loch lies like a heavenly mirror of blue. The sun blazes down on the bens and glens. The oars dip rhythmically as the boat breaks the glassy waters. The piper sits at the bow and sounds weird notes of gallantry and doom from shore to shore. The cuckoos flood the glens with their soft, elusive double-noted music, and the yellow-hammers laugh cheerily from the coppice on the shore. It is all so peaceful and placid.

But yonder above a little larch wood you can see a great Scots fir-tree towering into the sky. We land, and climb the steep hill, pushing a way through the dense twigs of the young larches, until, coming out on the top, we see the ancient Hanging Tree of the family standing on the tiny plateau. The hillock falls away on every side, and although to-day it is bearded by larches, yet this round, flat top looks wonderfully like an old Hill of Justice, on which this Hanging Tree has

G

stood for centuries. What ugly rows of dead men have hung from these level branches in the old, sad days ! What rattling of chains must have been heard on the dark nights when the wind blew the victims one against the other in a horrid dance of death ! Yet that was no uncommon sight near the house of a powerful chief like M'Shimie at Castle Doonie or M'Cailein at Castle Innerora. It is all by with now, that weird chapter of history. Cuckoos are calling to us on this perfect day of June. The larches send whiffs of heavenly scent through the little wood. The boat lies waiting on the shore. So, aboard again for another tale of Alastair the First.

His wife was Margaret Drummond. Drummond of Erinoch was the King's forester in the deer forest at the back of the Ben. One day he caught those nonesuch robbers, the Macgregors, stealing deer. Out flashed the steel, and the keepers killed the robbers. But the redheads did not forget. So back came other Macgregors, and murdered Drummond of Erinoch. They cut off his head, rolled it in a plaid, and came with it to the House of the Great Ben. The Stewart men were all away. So the Macgregors demanded food from Margaret Drummond. She gave them bread and cheese, and went out to fetch more. While she was away the red Macgregors set her father's head, all bloody, on the table, and stuffed the mouth with bread and cheese. When the Stewart lady came back, there surely was a sight to scare the soul of a saint ! With a cry she fled from the house, witless and demented, and took to the hills. Nor did she stop until she arrived at a little loch, which to this day is called *Lochan na Mna*, or the woman's loch. Night and day she spent on the hill, crying weirdly in the dark, and coming down only to get milk from the cows. Then she bore a son, who, according to tradition, was called the Major.

A man curiously moody in temperament because of the terrible circumstances of his birth, he became a namely fighter in the civil wars. Often had he to conceal himself from his enemies. Terrible in strength, he could squeeze the blood from the fingers of the man whose hand he grasped. Once, while sleeping in a hidie hole in a glen across the loch, he dreamed, three times over, that the rats were gnawing at the foundations of the House of the Great Ben. So he slipped across the loch in the dark and found a company of M'Ians harrying the place. Quickly he gathered his men. He saw his wife being compelled to open the byre doors to let out the cattle. Then the Major's sword sang. He killed the man who was compelling his wife, and did not halt till seven M'Ians were slain by his own sword arm. The seven bodies were dragged down to the shore with green withies and buried. Long years after, when the foundations of a new boathouse were being dug, and before the present shore road was made, the skeletons of the seven M'Ians were found. Now, you may rest yourself by an old gravestone on the shore and read the inscription : " Near this spot were interred the bodies of seven M'Donalds of Glencoe, killed when attempting to harry the House of the Great Ben—*Anno Domini* 1620."

It was this same Major Stewart who killed Lord Kilpont, the kinsman of the Great Montrose. Kilpont had commanded the bowmen who were on the left of Montrose at the Battle of Tippermuir, and that night, in the small hours, a quarrel arose between Kilpont and Stewart, who occupied the same tent. The reason for the *fracas* is still a puzzle of history. But Major Stewart stabbed Lord Kilpont to the heart, killed a sentry, and made off. For this he earned the hatred of the Grahams, and when he died, after a stormy life, his friends were so afraid lest the Grahams should commit an outrage on his body that they buried the Major—*shouchet* him in, as an old account has it—at the point of Coil-a-Mhor, where to-day you may stand at the Major's grave and read this inscription on the face of a grey, weather-beaten stone : " This stone marks the place of interment of Major James Stewart, afterwards removed to the family vault at Dundurn. Died about 1660."

A still quiet place is Dundurn now—that old ruined chapel of St Fillan the Leper, where the Major lies with all his ancient folk about him. Encircled by some of the sublimest hills in Scotland, the sons and daughters of the old house are still laid to sleep in this sweet hallowed spot.

But when you pass up the stair in the House of the Great Ben to your own sleeping place, you may touch the scabbard of the Major's sword where it hangs on the wall. You may handle the very claymore which he used when he slew the seven M'Ians. You may even slide your finger along the barrel of his famous *gunne breac*, or the spotted gun, which was his favourite weapon. It had such magic powers that it never missed its mark. The barrel is all spotted, and at one place a patch of silver gleams for two inches round the barrel, which is the oldest part of the gun. A famous gun was this *gunne breac*, and a bonny fighter was the moody Major. Indeed, the great Sir Walter has for ever enshrined him in the preface to *The Legend of Montrose*, and he is described in the romance as

Allan M'Aulay. The *gunne breac* was probably one of the first barrels imported into this country.

But in the summer twilight a hundred weapons gleam from the walls of the ancient hall and stairway. For, like all Highland gentlemen, the sons of the house went out in every age to many lands of battle, even until the year of the Great War, and like true children of the tartan, they always fell. Is not the battle march of the *Clann Stiubhartich* a cry to take the old highway of war—*Gabhaidh Sinn an Rathad-Mor* ?

> " Up the steep and heathery ben,
>   Down the bonny winding glen,
>   We march, a band of loyal men,
>   Let them say their will, O ! "

Highland claymores made by Andrea Ferrara. A steel cap bow with a gun stock. A Highland targe, covered with beautifully stamped leather, all brass-studded, with the original iron spike, $11\frac{1}{2}$ inches long, fixed in the brazen centre. But, rarest of all the wonders in this old armoury, a two-handed sword, with a four-foot blade, a handle $1\frac{1}{2}$ foot, and an original sheath, as old as the blade itself.

Sitting in the dim-lit room, with the sound of happy voices coming in at the open windows, it is strange to step back centuries as you handle that rare old crystal globe, the *Clach Dearg*. This clear rock crystal, which is about $1\frac{1}{2}$ inch in diameter, placed in a setting of four silver bands or slips, was long famous for its medicinal powers of curing disease in men and cattle. When dipped in water, a pink tinge comes over it. It is as dateless as it is mysterious. Nisbet, in his *System of Heraldry*, ascribes it to the middle of the fifteenth century. But, from the silver mountings, it

may date from the time of the Crusades. Many have
come to this House of the Great Ben and carried away
a pailful of charmed water, into which the magic *Clach
Dearg* has been dipped, and, like all ancient things of
magic, the *Clach Dearg* still thrills the fingers that
touch it.

The name of Stewart will for ever be associated
with the last romance of Prince Charles Edward, the
Tearlach Og so dear to Highland hearts. And from
this same House of the Great Ben there went out one
who was faithful to the Prince in his last broken days
at Rome. John Stewart, whom one of his contemporaries
called a rank Highlander, joined his Royal master in
1745, and was the only Scots attendant who was in his
intimate service to the end. He was the Prince's
major-domo, dressed his hair, excused his freedom
with the bottle, and looked after his private affairs.
Even the Cardinal of York, the Prince's brother, could
not part Charles and his faithful attendant. " There
are still two Britons with him, Mr Wagstaffe, an Englishman, and John Stewart, a Scotsman," wrote Oliphant
of Gask to Bishop Forbes when Charles had dismissed
his Scots attendants. The Prince died on 31st January
1788, and John Stewart attended him on his deathbed,
received a handsome legacy from him, married an
Italian lady, and himself died on a date unknown.
That was the end of an old song, and the last scene of
a deathless romance. His son became a colonel of
artillery in the Papal Guard.

If the walls of the old house could speak, what
other tales might not we hear of the gallant days when
men fought and women keened, when the children of
the mist were born to a heritage of strife, and the high
gests of life and love were all mixed with battle-cries !

LOCH RANNOCH : ST MICHAEL'S GRAVEYARD MARKED BY YEW TREES

But to-night, when the June darkness lies like a lambent twilight over the loch, the old house, and the Great Ben, the stillness is only broken by the whisper of waves on the shore. Suddenly, there is a sound of music, and the pipes fling out the challenge of that brave battle march, *Gabhaidh Sinn an Rathad Mor*—

> " We will take the good old way,
> Let them say their will, O ! "—

to the accompaniment of a little kettledrum, which wakes the dovering night hags in the trees and troubles the dead M'Ians down by the shore. Stillness again for a space. Then, the full moon rises above the hills, making a pathway of shimmering silver across the loch, and the pipes wail out the long notes of a lost tune with a sob in the chanter for the old days that will never be again.

XIII

THE ROAD TO RANNOCH

AND THE APPIN MYSTERY

THERE are many roads to Rannoch. But, whichever one a man takes he will find mystery at the end. For Rannoch has its secret, and Appin has its secret, and none may know them who is not content to take the bundle on the back and foot it for himself. A man may turn his face to the homely borderland, with its fine rivers and its fat fields, its Lowland Scots and its balladry—and he will carry with him all the way content and caution in his soul. But let him turn his face to the North, and once he has passed into the fastnesses of Atholl and Breadalbane he will take the Gaelic view of things, both old and new, when the mist swirls about him and the unutterable desolations of the mountains grip him like the fingers of some kilted cateran who springs, silent and sudden, on him from behind a rock in the glooms of Glencoe.

And yet, when I took the road on Culloden Day from Struan up the little glen of Errochty, the April sun was tempering the wind that blew icy-cold from the snow-capped peaks, and by the time I had dropped over the hill from Trinafour into Rannoch, the setting sun was reddening the dazzling cone of Schiehallion with a pink Alpine glow which was to herald in the warmest week of spring.

Next morning the sun was hot as midsummer, the winds had given over all their frolics and were still asleep, and the laughter of April was heard in every glade and glen. Sitting by the wood of Leargan, under a cloudless sky, the waters of the loch lay before me without a ripple, and the sharp peak of Schiehallion was reflected in the liquid mirror like a pearly plane taking a nose dive into the fathomless blue. Far away in the west the Shepherds of Etive and the Black Mount Hills made a white rampart to the world. The birch wood was a dream of transparency—a million silver barks gleaming against the steep carpet of russet leaves, the bare birken twigs making a purple mist of beauty above, with the blue sky breaking through. Whaups gurgled on the hill, oyster-catchers tu-leeped by the shore, a dog's bark across the loch sounded but a few yards away, and the full-fluted song of the blackbird was everywhere. Truly, a day of strength and stillness, love and beauty, hope and new beginnings, when

> " Ilka bird sang o' its luve,
> And fondly sae did I o' mine."

Somewhere in the deeps of the wood a hoolet blinked its blinded eyes in the blazing sun, and, forgetting that the time of day was only noon, hooted ridiculous as he dovered in his sleep. Then the little chanter dribbled out those notes of mystery which only a wandering man can call up from the deeps of time. For, on this day of ethereal beauty, nature was yielding herself up to the long languorous kiss of sunshine, which draws out all the love and life and laughter of the world.

Yonder across the water is Dall, with its Black Wood of old Caledonian Forest trees darkening the hillside by the shore—and yonder, in the gap between the virgin snows of Meal Muick and Ben Dearg, lies the larig—that fine hill-path which leads from Inner-wick in Glen Lyon to Dall in Rannoch.

At Killichonan Churchyard I sat down in the sun— to eat some bread and cheese, to register a disappoint-ment, and to remember a friend. The disappointment had to do with the unthinking zeal of someone in authority who has rebuilt the wall of this old church-yard. For, years ago (1910), I took a sketch, which I have before me now, of an ancient holy-water boulder-font which was built into a square recess in the wall by the gate. Now the mason has abolished altogether this ancient shrine, and I found the little font lying on a stone in the grass inside the wall, without protec-tion, and in danger of being mistaken for a stone of no importance. May Heaven defend us from all such local restorations. The remembered friend was one who was brought here from a town far in the South to find, after great suffering, her last resting-place among her own clan—now all gone. So, sitting in the sun by Killichonan Kirkyard, memory calls forth old sorrows bravely borne—for the greatest things on the travelling road are the friends we meet and the burdens we share.

Then come the yellow sands of Camusericht glisten-ing in the heat ; the little tower standing out of the water on *Eilean nam Faoileag*, Isle of Storms ; Rannoch Barracks with its sough of the '45 ; and the seven miles of rough road due west from the loch to Rannoch Station. Once while sheltering there beneath the trees, in a downpour of rain, a little squirrel came right down the trunk of a pine-tree and looked into the face of the motionless man whose eyelids never quivered.

APPIN : OLD KIRK AND GRAVEYARD

So still, so innocent, so near was the furry creature, that I heard it hiss out question after question in a voice which made a sound like *quince-quince*.

Now we are nearing the mystery of the moor. The wild tumbling waters of the Gaur River keep company with the road most of the way, until the river slides out of Loch Eigheach. There is a fine viewpoint from the hill where the old grassy track leaves the new road near the Falls of Gaur. Here you get the first impression of that waste of great rocks and stones which spreads over the whole moor, like a curse, and gives it an unearthly sense of desolation. At Rannoch Station the wan waters of Loch Laidon gleam in the sun, and just a little way from the iron rails begins the path which leads along Loch Laidon to Kingshouse. For the first four or five miles the path wanders more or less along the loch to a shepherd's cottage—Tigh-na-Cruach—now empty. Then it strikes across the hillside for another five miles to Black Corries, from which a fairly good road leads to Kingshouse Inn, three miles distant. There was some word of the county authorities of Argyll and Perth opening up this path as a regular road, but the financial troubles of these present times have made that project a dream of the future.

To-day we set out for Bridge of Orchy. The great rock masses which make the Bounds of Rannoch, from Buchaille Etive to Clachlet, from Stob Gobhair to Ben Dorain, are like the crystal gates of heaven, glistening white in the sun. The moor itself—a waste of twenty miles square—is to-day a veritable painters' palette, covered with brown madders and every shade of burnt sienna, with here and there bright splashes of yellow ochre, where the mosses and saxifrages are already putting on their little robes of spring. The

altar fires of burning heather send up pillars of blue
smoke far away, where the hills at the head of Glen
Lyon slope down to the eastern confines of the moor.
The deer are feeding in Crannoch Wood among the
old forest trees. The long light day dies with a tranquil
sunset. At Bridge of Orchy, where kind hearts have
never failed, the evening star hung in solitary splendour
like a silver lamp above the white gleam of Ben Dorain,
and the husheen of the river made a music which is
the finest prelude to dreams.

The thirteen miles from the Bridge of Orchy to
Kingshouse make a wild, rough road, and land you in
the eeriest part of the moor. Round Loch Tulla and
up behind the woods of Black Mount, it skirts the foot
of Ben Toaig, and you are only half-way across when
you reach Ba Bridge. Here is a resting-place which is
always hard to pass by. For you look right up the
brawling stream into Corrie Ba, the forest sanctuary.
The great white summits of Stob Gobhair, Aonach
Mhor, and Clachlet stand to-day like glittering sentries
that none may challenge, and somewhere in the deeps
of that corrie the stags and hinds wander free. On a
day in August 1914, a few hours before the Great
War was declared, I lay on the summit of Stob Gobhair
(3565 feet), just before a rainstorm burst. The clouds
and mountains were as black as ink, and the wild world
was as still as death. The corrie was like a bottomless
pit, and somewhere in the black silence far below a
great stag yawned. Then the storm burst, and for
hours the opened heavens sent down a merciless, sting-
ing rain. It was a parable of events—for the very
next day we heard that the black clouds of war had
burst in Belgium, bringing darkness and death to
Europe for years to come.

But to-day Corrie Ba is a sanctuary of peace. The stream tumbles below the old bridge. The deer bound across the road, hungry and unafraid. A little wagtail sits bobbing on the parapet. Clachlet lifts its pearly peak into the blue. Farther up the road a solitary tramp sits by a stream gutting little trout which he has guddled in a pool, to broil on a fire for his midday meal. The time of day is our only introduction. April sunshine, the simple meal, the sweet, new-caught fish, and the vasty views across the moor—here is the happy life and the friendly road, from which one regains a simple faith in human nature and forgets the cares of a weary world.

At a bridge above Ba Cottage take your stand and look eastward. The mysterious beauty of the moor lies all before you now, with the waters of Loch Buidhe, Loch-na-Stainge, Loch-na-Hachlaise, Loch Ba, the bends of the river, and a hundred other little blue lochans studding the tawny bosom of the moor like sapphires set in brown velvet. The road now rises to a height of 1449 feet, and sweeps down to Kingshouse in a mass of gravel, where a squad of men are repairing a washout which took place during the winter snows and rains. Yonder rises the noble rock-face of Buchaille Etive, away to the north is Black Corries Lodge, and here is Kingshouse, with the stone-strewn moor and a glimpse of Loch Laidon.

A murderous spot is Kingshouse when the mist is abroad and the night falls ominous. But even on a blue day like this the moor grips you with a sense of eeriness. A crouching form seems to hide behind each of these myriad rocks, the refuse of a glacier age, which lie scattered over the vast wilderness. An intolerable silence reigns. Faint airs whisper about the ears. A bird cries piteously far out on the moor—lost, lonely, appropriate. The very inn, with its scrunty trees, is evil-looking and lifeless. The green door, all scarred and pock-marked with the weather, is on this fine day inhospitably locked. So the by-goer has to chap for a refreshment.

What deeds have been done of old at Kingshouse ! Red-coated soldiers hunting the clansmen ; wild caterans in ragged tartans driving a creach of lowing cattle ; the Campbell soldiers coolly cantering to the massacre of the M'Ians down-by ; men like Colkitto Macdonald, Col of the Cows, as that king of thieves was called, the chosen guide of Viscount Dundee through Lochaber ; gentlemen of fortune like Alan Breck and John Splendid—one and all and many such passed a night at Kingshouse, with dirk and pistol handy by the pillow. Here we are in the very centre of the mystery of Rannoch. But surely Robert Louis Stevenson was drawing over bravely on his fancy when he made a regiment of horse sweep that moor, for it is full of deathly bogs and impassable peat hags !

As the road leads us away from the ghosts of Kingshouse we plunge into the wild Pass of Glencoe, where the mountains oppress the solitary traveller. It is an ill place for a Scot to pass through, this same Glen of Weeping, if he happens to have a clinging memory for the treacheries of a Campbell or the heartless cruelties of a Stair. Not all the precipices of Bidean nor the cave high up on Aonach Dubh can keep him from looking long at the little glen behind Clachaig. In fearful fancy, he hears those cries of anguish at five o'clock in the morning, and sees the smoke of the burning houses in the snow, where thirty-eight Macdonalds, including two children, two women, and an old man of eighty, were murdered in cold blood by men who had partaken of their hospitality.

But to-day the sun is shining, and the seawrack is already scenting the winds that blow from Loch Leven. Up there in Carnoch, by the Bridge of Coe, an old man—a Cameron—taught me to play a melodeon when I was a boy. Yonder, on St Munda's Isle, with its mysterious graves, I have seen the ghostly lights. And here, at Ballachulish Ferry, we are in Appin proper. With thoughts of another shameful miscarriage of justice we climb the little Gallows Hill above the Ferry and read, by the light of the sunset, this inscription on the monument, which stands as a non-committal but complete indictment of a clan that is not named : "*Erected in* 1911 *to the memory of James Stewart of Acharn, or James of the Glens, executed on this spot, Nov.* 8, 1752, *for a crime of which he was not guilty.*"

I am never in Appin but I try to fathom the Appin Mystery—"Who killed the Red Fox?" It is an over-adventurous question. For the shooting of Campbell of Glenure in the Wood of Lettermore yonder is still the hundred-and-fifty-year-old Mystery of Appin. I tried again this year. But in every case the man interrogated smiled and said he did not know. It was Andrew Lang who said that the tragedy remains as fresh in the memory of the people of Appin and Lochaber as if it were an affair of yesterday, and he adds—"I have had the secret—the secret which I may not tell." And one of the latest historians of the affair tells us that the true story of the Appin Murder is known to at least one family, who have preserved their secret inviolate. Certain it is—that Alan Breck, "the pock-marked," did not fire the shot : that James

Stewart of Acharn, or Seumas a Ghlinne, did not commit the murder for which he was hanged ; that several were in the planning of the affair ; and that a man with a short dark-coloured coat was seen escaping along the hillside carrying a gun. This man in the short coat—the mysterious other man—escaped. There, you have the mystery of the Appin murder, which still is expressed in this single question—" Who killed the Red Fox ? "

As I was wandering in a place of Appin I met an old man with the Gaelic tradition in his soul, and the Celt's long memory that never forgets— and, at long last, he told me the secret. I now know the name of the man who killed the Red Fox. I know the house where, until recently, there lay the *gunne dubh a mhifhortain*—the black gun of the misfortune. I know, also, why and where the fatal gun will never now be found. But, strangest of all, I too, when asked for the secret, can only smile like the men of Lochaber and the men of Appin, and say, " I may not tell ! "

In the old kirkyard of Appin there are some rare Stewart memorials.

There is, in a rough shrine, the boulder gravestone from Culloden, with the four words on it, *Clan Stewart of Appin*, and this moving inscription carved above—" This old stone, removed to Appin 1906, originally stood at the head of the grave on Culloden Moor, where lie 92 officers and men of the Stewarts of Appin, who fell in the memorable charge of the right wing of the Prince's army, April 16, 1746."

There is also an old marble grave slab with the following quaint record on it—" Here lie the remains of James Stewart, Esq., of Fassnacloich, and Janet M'Donald, daughter to Alexander M'Donald of

Glencoe, his spouse, by whom he had twenty-two children." (No date.)

Still a third stone rejoices in this scriptural gem— " Sacred to the memory of Ann Stewart, the amiable wife of the Rev. Donald M'Coll, 15th September, 1810. Delightful Ann, in Abraham's bosom filled with many a saint."

To those wife Celts who can read between the lines let these stones speak.

Beneath a mighty spruce-tree of Barcaldine I lit the last roadside fire, with primroses on every side. Willow-warblers, robins, and blackbirds sang about me. A pheasant sounded its hollow challenge in a dingle of the wood. The whaups whistled and wailed far up the hill. Down by the shore the gulls kept complaining, and in the wood itself, high up among the tree-tops, the wind made a sound like distant sea-waves. The fire sent its pungent blue reek into the sunlit air. No living soul came by. Somewhere there must be towns and cities where men are ettling after siller with jealous hearts and puckered brows. Certain it is that one telephone bell rings in vain far away. But here, secure in the thought that not a soul on earth knows exactly where I am, the little pipe dribbles out a pibroch of everlasting good-byes, which only the rabbits and the dovering birds can hear—and after the tune is over, a strong man's laughter mingles with the laughter of spring.

On the open roads of the world there is just one thing finer than anything in nature. It is the sense of human brotherhood which makes one tramp share with another his bread or his matches, his little broiled trout, or his homely conversation. There are kind hearts in every Highland glen and on every Lowland

H

road. To those who gave happy hospitality under the lofty roof-tree, or by the little peat fire, which never goes out—to those who made the long road seem short with the best of company and the adventurous question, meeting as wandering folk in the Glen of Weeping, and parting on the braes of Kentallen, with a twist of regret—to those, too, who told their secrets which will never be betrayed—to one and all be blessing, and a hundred thousand welcomes at the next meeting on the long white road which stretches out before us for ever and a day.

XIV

THE BOUNDS OF BLACK MOUNT

AN IDYLL OF THE RED-DEER

As with sweethearts, so with places. No lover can say that he knows the one or the other until he has been so often that he has lost count of his visits. So is it with the clachan that lies below the corrie at the back of Ben Dorain. For me there is always a light at the window in a long, low roof-tree on the darkest night, and the door is never closed when I knock. The returning has become a habit of the heart, and I have long ago lost count.

Bridge of Orchy is a mere handful of houses which are bielded by a narrow strip of trees on a steep brae between the station and the river. Add to the loneliness a breath of resin from the little pines, a whiff of peat-reek from the kitchen fires, salmon in the river, red-deer on the hill, a shop, a post office, and a policeman, and what more could any reasonable man wish for? The road sweeps over an old soo-backit bridge, and turns sharply to the right up the brawling river. If you were to follow that road for ever and a day you would not grow tired of what lies beyond, for it leads you right into the heart of the most desolate moor in Scotland, and takes you to the uttermost bounds of the Black Mount Forest, from Rannoch to Etive, from Glencoe to Glenorchy. If you come in January you will find nothing but pearly peaks of snow and ice

fretting the blue of the wintry skies. Even in April
the snows are still in perfect condition on the high
tops and in the corries for step-cutting and the climbers'
craft ; but the river tumbles in early spate between
tawny banks that are already whispering of spring ;
and in May you will find primrose tufts in the woods
about Forest Lodge. To-day, in this blazing month
of July, the great hills are greener than I have ever
seen them, the station is framed in yellow broom, and
soon the heather will be purple to the very doors.
Come in late October and you will see the fires of
autumn burning the woods and hills all red and gold,
and if you are belated on the road in the gloaming the
stags will be sending their bellow and roar into the
mouth of eerie night.

Travel north or south, you must always pass over
the old Brig. Stewarts, Camerons, M'Ians, and
Campbells, with many a man of smaller name forby,
have often been glad to win the other side of this same
Brig. I never put my elbows on the parapet and
look down stream but I think of the signal which
John Splendid saw lying on the glenside keystone
when he was showing a clean pair of heels after Inverlochy. Three sprigs of gall, a leaf of ivy, a bare twig
of oak standing up at a slant, and a peeled willow
withy, one end of which pointed in the direction of the
Glen—the whole held together by two stones. Here
was a message that might well have bamboozled the
best of scouts—and yet it was clear enough. For the
three sprigs of gall meant three Campbells ; the oak
leaf meant a Stewart who was always reminding the
Campbells that his race was royal ; the ivy meant a
Gordon ; the peeled withy clearly spelled men in a
hurry ; and the oak branch pointed to the position of

the sun.   Five fugitives of these names hurrying south
over the Brig of Orchy at three o'clock in the afternoon !
That is the kind of scoutcraft which is to-day a lost
art, something that is far beyond a city-bred man with
towny brains.

There are two ways from Bridge of Orchy to
Inveroran—one by the road along the shores of Loch
Tulla, the other over the shoulder of Inverveigh by
the old drove road which you can still trace in the
heather.   Go the one way and come back the other ;
rest yourself in the hospitable inn at Inveroran, whose
tea-table you will find groaning with all the home-made
blessings ; and you will never regret it.   As you mount
the heather you marvel at the fine broad highway which
must once have been here.   The track is rather elusive
at certain places, and it is sometimes difficult to keep to
it.   But at the top of the hill it is well defined, and another
hill road strikes straight south-west for the summit of
Inverveigh.   Stand here, and if the day is fine, you will
sweep the glories of Black Mount with a lover's eye.

That little green ridge below you on the other side of
Glen Euar is Druimliart, where Duncan Ban Macintyre
—Duncan of the Songs, the hunter bard of Glenorchy
—lived long ago.   Ben Dorain was his own hill—

> " The honour o'er each hill
>   Hath Ben Dorain."

And with Donnachadh Ban the red-deer were a perfect
passion—

> " And sweeter to my ear
>   Is the concert of the deer
>   In their roaring,
>   Than when Erin from her lyre
>   Warmest strains of Celtic fire
>   May be pouring ;

H 2

> And no organ sends a roll
> So delightful to my soul
> As the branchy-crested race
> When they quicken their proud pace
> And bellow in the face
>   Of Ben Dorain."

Above Druimliart, and just beyond Clashgour, in Glen Dochard, you can see the silver sheen of Loch Dochard. Over all that wonderful panorama on this sweltering July day the great mountains rise like giants thrusting their heads into the sky. Ben Staray, the Rough Hill (3541); Stob Coir' 'an Albannaich, the Highlandman's Peak (3425); Stob Gobhair, the Hill of Goats (3565); then shapely Ben Toaig (2712) behind the Lodge, with Clachlet, the Stone Hill (3602) peeping over its shoulder: a glimpse of the Glencoe Bens, the whole range of Rannoch Moor sweeping eastwards to Ben Achallader (3404), Ben Dothaidh (3283), and Ben Dorain (3524); with Loch Tulla lying below you in the centre of the picture, sparkling in the sun like a shimmering mirror. These, with some lesser hills, make the blessed Bounds of Black Mount. You may not climb them all. But if you would walk the Bounds you must go up by Loch Dochard, down Glenkinglass, till you sniff the brown seawrack on Lock Etive, then up the lochside, through Glen Etive, to Kingshouse, and over the Rannoch Moor road by the sanctuary of Corrie Ba to Bridge of Orchy.

What a wealth of memories rise within me as I gaze! Yonder, beyond the gleaming sands at the head of Loch Tulla, stand the ruins of Achallader Castle. It was at Achallader that John Glas, first Earl of Breadalbane, who was described as being " cunning as a fox, wise as a serpent, and as slippery as an eel," met the Highland chiefs with power to distribute a sum of £15,000 among them to secure their loyalty to King William's Government. The money was a political bait, but into whose pockets it went no one will ever be quite sure. M'Ian of Glencoe held out to the last, but, as all the world knows, he was too late, and Captain Robert Campbell of Glen Lyon, under Major Robert Duncanson, set out one cold winter day in February 1692 with his murder men to massacre the Macdonalds.

Other memories, more pleasant and more personal, rise up—memories of days spent on some of these high tops, from Stob Gobhair to Ben Dorain, in sunshine and rain, in snow and mist, in summer and winter. Long lambent nights, spent by the Lady's Pool on the Orchy or by the pool below the falls on the Kinglass, watching the salmon leaping in the broken water, until the sun went down and we could no longer see the play. Hot hours spent up in the corrie between Dorain and Dothaidh, plunging into the caller pools of the little mountain burn again and again, and then sitting down in the sun to read some classic page—full-dressed in a pair of spectacles. Standing on Ben Dorain's topmost ridge, looking down on Loch Lyon with long, wistful thoughts of St Adamnan, who came to this wild barrier of Drumalbain Hills in the seventh century. Stravaiging at a loose end, all alone, on the wastes of Rannoch Moor :

> " Who has the hills for friend
> Has a God-speed to end
>   His path of lonely life
> And wings of golden memory."
>   —GEOFFREY WINTHROP YOUNG.

One of the beauties of Black Mount to me is the wealth of old Caledonian Forest trees which you will find in Crannach Wood and in Doire Darrach on the shores of Loch Tulla. Time was when the country was covered with them. But for centuries we have only been able to infer this from the fact that in the peat mosses of Rannoch Moor and elsewhere have been found great roots. I have made a fire in a corrie 1500 feet up, on a perfectly safe place in the wet hagg, with red pine roots taken out of the peat. It is the finest fuel in the world. The smoke mingled with the creeping mists and so hid the whereabouts of the fire. I lit my pipe with the blazing root of a tree under which one of Ossian's heroes or St Adamnan himself may have sat to rest himself. But why did all these forests in Scotland disappear and die out? The theory that they were ruthlessly cut down by the ancient inhabitants of Caledonia is quite inadequate. Might it not rather have been some great Peat Age that arose to kill them out, and then preserve their remains when they fell into the great bogs? We know that sheep and deer eat away the young seedlings. This has been proved by an experiment for which, if I mistake not, Lady Breadalbane was responsible some years ago down yonder in Doire Darrach, by the side of Loch Tulla. Four separate groups of old forest trees were fenced in to keep the deer and sheep from eating the natural seedlings. The result is seen to-day within these four fenced spaces, where round about each giant are growing healthy young seedlings in a natural disarray, and not in formal patches like ordinary plantations, one of which you will see nearer Inveroran Inn. These ancient Caledonian pines are one of the few ancient glories of Scotland remaining to us, but their disappearance in olden times is a perpetual mystery, whose solution I leave to others.

Being no fisher in the orthodox sense, but a man who employs his own original methods if need be, I will say nothing of the fine trout of Loch Tulla, Loch Ba, Lochan na h-Achalise, and Loch Buidhe. But the red-deer fill the soul of a mountain lover with a strong desire which is ill to deny. Great desolations of crag and glen, remote feeding-places, the sound of distant streams, wind and rain and burning sun, wild life studied at first hand, long days in the heather and heavenly nights on the tops—red-deer mean all that (and much more that is secret) to the wandering man. What is true of one forest is true of all. It is such a fine adventure. A very cautious peep over the edge of a rock is followed by a sudden drop on to the hands and knees or a creep to a safe coign of vantage. There they are at last! Ten, twenty, fifty of them, feeding quietly up the hollow in the sun. The stags walk majestically in front, or in the middle of the hinds, which glide with an indescribable grace from one feeding place to another, while the little calves trot timorously by their side. The heat is terrific—but so is desire in the heart of man. Oh, the glamour of a pair of antlers appearing over the skyline or the green lip of a balloch! Then another and another. On they come in single file at first, then in twos and threes. Across a bit of burnt heather they glide like a brown cloud, with the sun blazing on their ruddy flanks. Then one stag lies down to rest in the heather. Another moves quietly on. Two hinds run to a little stream to drink. A tiny calf farther off has evidently lost its mother hind, and in the silence, across the hot still pass, comes the hollow cry of *maw-maw* from the wandered baby deer, to be answered by the anxious *snort-snort* of the hind. Another calf is drinking in its mother's milk with a tranquil relish. What a romance of wild life seen at close quarters many a time by a single pair of human eyes, remote from all the haunts of men! But now the big stag is up and looking straight this way. The wind has changed. He sniffs a taint on the slight breeze that has arisen to temper the heat. The presence of that dangerous intruder, man, has been detected. The signal is given, silently and mysteriously as only a stag can give it; and his wives, who have been well trained to obedience, follow him at the double, up and over the pass which leads to the ever-welcome sanctuary of the corrie or the wood.

The glamour of the deer forest is something far more wonderful than the mere pursuit of a quarry or the killing of a stag. It takes a jaded man back to the primitive pleasures of long days on the hill, wide and elusive visions, the breath of mountain winds, with all the natural joys of strenuous effort and sporting adventure. The petty things that tease the soul in crowded streets and the airless flats of the world are left far below the wandering man as he stands on the high tops and trains his eye to infinite horizons of land and sea where heaven and earth become one in the blue mists of distance. For one who has never stalked a stag and is never likely to shoot one, the red-deer of Scotland have become a passion of the heart. I once had a gallant troop of Boy Scouts—all, alas! grown up now, and some making good sleep in the graves of Flanders and France. One of the patrols was a stag patrol, and, needless to say, every boy in it could roar to the life like a twelve-pointer! Moreover, the red-deer teach us many arts of life which the foolish never learn—to efface ourselves ; to move as silently as a snake without disturbing our neighbours ; and to love nature with such an intimate knowledge that we know how to take the very winds unseen into our confidence.

" Oh, I wadna' be a clerk, mither, to bide aye ben,
    Scrabbling ower the sheets o' parchment wi' a weary, weary pen,
    Looking thro' the lang stane windows at a narrow strip o' sky,
    Like a laverock in a withy cage, until I pine away and die.

      ·   ·   ·   ·   ·   ·   ·

    So I'm aff and away to the muirs, mither, to hunt the deer,
    Ranging far frae frowning faces and the douce folk here.

      ·   ·   ·   ·   ·   ·   ·

    Oh, the wafts o' heather honey and the music o' the brae
    As I watch the great harts feeding, nearer, nearer, a' the day !

      ·   ·   ·   ·   ·   ·   ·

    Ye'll bury me 'twixt the brae and the burn in a glen far away,
    Where I may hear the heathcock craw and the great harts bray ;
    And gin my ghaist can walk, mither, I'll go glowering at the sky
    The live-long night on the black hillside where the dun deer lie."
                      —CHARLES KINGSLEY.

XV

THE LOCH OF THE VANISHED RACES

A RUNE OF RANNOCH

THERE is nothing gloomy about it, for the great hills
lie far back from its shores and let the sun and wind
play freely about its open waters. Indeed, from the
bright, wave-washed beach at Kinloch to the far-off
Glencoe Bens the west winds race helter-skelter over
the great moor with its desolate lochans, down the
gorge of the Gaur River, and over ten clear miles of
sparkling water, until you begin to think of Loch
Rannoch as the loch of perpetual breezes. It gives you
the sense of the open sea as few inland Highland lochs
do. The shapely cone of Schiehallion guards its eastern
shores, and the dim blue Shepherds of Etive stand
sentinel in the sunset far away.

And yet, this heartsome Highland loch, for all its
beauty and brightness, will always be to me the Loch
of the Vanished Races. For round its shores there is
a chain of ancient graves, many a dead village, and a
whole world of lost romance, the very sough of which
can only be heard by those who know how to lean a
fond ear to the pipes of time as they wail sad coronachs
down the glens. It may be that the Celt has not yet
reached his last horizon in this grey old land. But, at
least, no one who has haunted the Hebrid Isles, wandered
in the waste places of the hills, or looked long and

lovingly for some news of a lost folk in the Standing
Stones can deny that where once the glens were thick
with clansmen and hundreds rallied to the battle-cry,
to-day it would be hard to enlist a company or gather
a mere platoon. The wind sings only one lament as it
moans about the bracken braes where the shielings lie
in ruins :

CHA TILL, CHA TILL, CHA TILL MI TUILLE.
No more, no more, no more returning.

Standing any summer day in the little square at
Kinloch, you will hear nothing but the clatter of English
tongues, with a word or two of the good Gaelic wafted
to you on a stray breeze when a bodach goes by or a
ghillie passes on to the smiddy, with a garron from
Tummelside or far Corrievachtie. Yet, time was
when the shores of Rannoch swarmed with Robertsons,
Macgregors, and Camerons, with some venturesome
Campbells who had travelled north from the real
Argyll.

There is a rocky height above Kinloch called
Craigievar, once tree-clad, now bare and bald except
for a tuft of pines left on its summit, like the feathers
on an Indian's head. Climb the scarp, and what a
volume of history you can read in that little open valley
—once an extension of the Loch—which runs from the
river mouth to Dunalastair !

Yonder, snuggling among the trees at the glen-
foot right opposite is Innerhadden, where St Chad
is said to have had a *disert* or chapel of retreat. This
is more than likely. For, when Aidan, that princely
successor of Columba in Iona, went south to Lindis-
farne, he brought back from Northumbria two of his

Saxon converts, the brothers Cedd and Chad, to receive
further instruction in Iona. When they were on their
return journey, some time about 650, they settled for
a time at Fortingal in the Lyon Valley, beyond Schiehallion, and while there St Cedd built churches at
Fortingal and Logierait, while his brother St Chad
founded the churches of Grandtully and Foss. Both
were made bishops on their return to the south. St Cedd
was Bishop of Essex, and St Chad fixed his See of
Mercia at Lichfield, where in the Cathedral to-day you
can look upon his shrine.

How much meaning there is in an ancient Gaelic
word! As Innerhadden means the Beginning of the
Fight, and Dalchosnie means the Field of Victory, and
Glen Sassunn that runs between them means the
Englishman's Glen, I see here a complete place-name
description of the Battle of Innerhadden, which took
place in the year 1306. That was the momentous
year when Robert Bruce killed John Comyn within the
chapel of the Minorites at Dumfries in February, was
crowned King at Scone in March, and was defeated
at Methven by the English under the Earl of Pembroke
in June. All through the summer night Bruce and his
followers fled across the hills to Atholl, until the morning
found them tired and hungry, in a wood on Tummelside, near Killiecrankie. A woman was making porridge
in a house close by, and Bruce asked for some of the
fine brose. So the wood was called ever after *Coille
Brochain*, the Wood of the Brose, and a gable of the
old house still stands with a tablet in the wall, on which
is carved this legend: " Robert the Bruce rested here
after the Battle of Methven—1306." An old site on
the Tummel hillside across the river from Dunalastair
and a little east from Macgregor's Cave is still known

as *Seomar-an-righ*, the Room of the King. Doubtless one of Bruce's haunts, for he hid for a time in Rannoch. But his enemies found him out, and a battle was fought between Innerhadden and Dalchosnie. Bruce gained the victory and the English fled south over the hills by the nearest glen. So, in these three Gaelic place-names—Innerhadden, Dalchosnie, and Glen Sassunn—we have the whole history of this battle in brief : the Beginning of the Fight, the Field of Victory, and the Glen of the English. It is said that the women of Lassentullich, that Hill of Passion near by, were so anxious to help Bruce that they took off their stockings, filled them with stones, and laid on ferociously whenever an Englishman came near.

At Lassentullich you can still see the ancient chapel of St Blane on the rock above the road, with a grave-yard behind. Little Norman windows pierce the ruined walls, a tiny holy-water font lies in the recess of the churchyard wall, and a fine old Celtic cross on an upright slab stands near the gate — all eloquent of the old Faith. Here, also, was St Peter's Well, and doubtless the neighbouring place called Tempar commemorates some *Tom-Peadar*, or Hill of Peter. There used to stand a large stone in a field west of Tempar Lodge, called the *Clach Sgoilt* or Split Stone, until it was broken up for road-metal—so I am told. For when the Stewarts of Innerhadden went out to fight for Prince Charlie, a Stewart woman who lived here heard on Culloden day a black dog howling most pitifully, and then by some strange occult force this great stone was suddenly split in two. She knew then that her man was dead, and there was keening in Rannoch that day. What a weird world of love and lore can be reaped from a few old Gaelic words !

But it is graves and dead chieftains all the way. You can stand high up in the burial ground of the Stewarts of Innerhadden, among the trees, and look east to Dunalastair. You can stand among dead Macdonalds at St Blanes of Lassentullich and look through the little window to Loch Garry's House across the Tummel. You come next to an old derelict burial place of the Stewarts of Crossmount across the road below the lodge, where the view westward was once open, before the trees grew up. You cross the bridge over the river at the gorge of Dunalastair, and, if you know where to find it, you can climb through the wood to the little enclosure where the old Struan Robertsons of Rannoch sleep below the lordly new house of Dunalastair, the ancient Mount Alexander of the clan. A stone's-throw farther and you come to St Luke's burial-ground where Robertsons, Camerons, and Campbells sleep peacefully enough now. Above them stands the new cross of a new laird, on a new mound. But the old Struans sleep to-day beneath long grass and nettles.

If you would view the home of the Struan Robertsons of the Clan Donnachie, that ancient family which descended from the last of the Earls of Athole who lived at the end of the thirteenth century, you must recross the bridge and ascend the mossy path through the wood on the south side of the Tummel to the rocky height called Macgregor's Cave. I doubt if any Macgregor ever spent a night in this luxurious cave, with its built lean-to against the rock, its window and doors, its flat resting slabs, its drain-pipe chimney in the roof, and its old tiles. But there is a cave below on the river bank where these red-headed outlaws may very well have lived.

The view from the Macgregor's Cave west, up
Rannoch to Glencoe, and east, down Tummel to Ben
Vrackie, is superb. Opposite, stands the stately modern
house of Dunalastair on its green terraces overlooking
the swirling black pools of the river. There is now a
dam here, but it is of old Struan and his ancient hermitage that we sit and dream, up here, with Schiehallion
at our backs and the incomparable valley of Tummel
below, all blazing with purple heather.

Struan was the beau-ideal of a Jacobite laird.
Born in 1668, he died in 1749 at the age of 81, and
he was " out " three times for the Royal Stuarts.
This gay young adventurer fought first at Killiecrankie
in 1689, and thereafter spent thirteen years as an
exile on the Continent, where he lived the happy-go-
lucky life of many another poor but proud Highland
gentleman, kicking his heels at fortune and wearying
for Dunalastair. His sister Margaret, who stayed at
home in Rannoch, was the guardian angel of his life.
She went up to Queen Anne and got her gallant brother
pardoned, and in 1703 the masterful Jacobite laird
of 35 returned to his hermitage on Tummel, only
to be deprived of his estates when the Queen died.
It was then that the little house at Carie was built
on a sunny spit of land with its windows looking straight
down the loch to Dunalastair.

But Struan was out again in the 1715 Rebellion,
taking 500 of the clan to fight with him under the
Earl of Mar. At Sheriffmuir he was taken prisoner,
and soon found himself locked up in Edinburgh Castle.
But Margaret Robertson never failed him. She organ-
ised a strong party of Robertsons and led them in a
secret sortie against the Castle, and once more Struan
was free. Eight years more were spent as an exile in

I

Holland and France, until his health broke down in Orleans in the year 1723. Once again Margaret, who was now a beautiful woman of 57, with pure white hair, went up to London and pled with King George to pardon the sick exile and allow him to return to his native air. The King was overcome by her beauty and her appeal, and allowed the inveterate Jacobite to return, but he stipulated that the estates were to be given to Struan's sister, not to himself.

This gay Cavalier, who was a poet as well as a soldier, went to Bath on his return and took the cure. One strict injunction was laid upon him by Dr Cheyne —that henceforth he was to have nothing to do with women. So, under the care of his sister, he returned to Dunalastair and straightway expelled every woman from the estate except those of his own family. On the entrance gate he fixed up a notice which ran thus :

> " In this small spot whole paradise you'll see
>   With all its plants but the forbidden tree ;
>   Here every sort of animal you'll find
>   Subdued, but woman, who betrayed mankind."

This placard caused great consternation among the ladies of his acquaintance, who pouted their lips and called Struan the Great Solitaire.

But he was an ill man to bind, and when Prince Charlie unfurled the standard in 1745, old Struan, at the age of 77, was " out " again. He bared his head at Glenfinnan before the Prince and said, " I devoted my youth to your grandsire, my manhood to your father, and now I offer my old age to your Royal Highness." This game old Highland gentleman actually fought at Prestonpans, but was not allowed to continue the campaign. In honour of his gallantry, however, he was sent home to Rannoch in Sir John Cope's war chariot, dressed in Cope's fur-lined coat and wearing his gold chain. The chariot was driven all the way from Edinburgh, and where the Highland roads become impossible, it was drawn by relays of horses and Robertson clansmen.

After Culloden Struan fled to Carie House. He had often to hide up Carie Burn. Here, in his last years, the old Jacobite warrior gave himself up to religion, tended by his faithful sister, and gazing daily out of the little windows which looked down the loch to Dunalastair. He died on 18th April 1749, an old, fiery-souled man of 81. The funeral was the largest ever seen in Rannoch, for the Chief was followed by 2000 clansmen and friends to his burial-place at the Kirk of Struan.

Those were the days when there were still some wolves in Rannoch. Struan hunted them down until there was only one great dog-wolf left. This brute was all the more to be feared because it was a baby-stealer, and had destroyed several children. To-day there is a lonely little farm in a hollow of the moors below the Struan road which is called Mullinavadie. Here in olden times there was a meal-mill. One day the miller's wife was mashing potatoes in the kitchen with her wooden bittle. The grey wolf walked in and made straight for the cradle, in which lay a six-months'-old baby. The Robertson woman raised her bittle and hit the wolf behind the ear, killing it on the spot. The head was afterwards cut off by her goodman and sent as a gift to Struan, and the place is called to this day *Mullinavadie*—the Mill of the Wolf.

Walk round the loch and you will find the same story of lost lore and a vanished race of heroes. The standing-stone in the garden of Loch Rannoch Hotel is called *Clach-a-Mharscin*, the Stone of the Pedlar, because a packman once sat down to rest himself against it, threw his pack over the stone, and was strangled by the strap. On the shore below Annet there is a grave. Here lies the last Rannoch man who was hanged for sheep-stealing. He dangled in chains from that great oak-tree close-by which has four trunks and some fine handy horizontal branches. Climb the hill above Annet itself and you will find the remains of a large village. I counted twenty-four distinct houses, and there are many more stone heaps where other houses probably stood. Yonder by the wood at Leargan is the only cottage left of this hillside community. Past this ancient village runs a very old right-of-way to Loch Garry, and the story is that there was a sudden raid down this old war-path from the north, and the whole village was left tenantless and deserted. The cloverstones had just been gathered from the fields in preparation for further husbandry, and there they are to-day, mute reminders of the breathless haste of the fugitives.

There must have been a holy cell or chapel here, for the very name of *Annait* means a relic chapel. The Annait was the church where the patron-saint was educated, or in which he kept his relics, and it ranked first among the different kinds of chapel. Is there not a *Bal-na-hanait* over yonder in Glen Lyon, a *Tobar-na-hanait* in Skye, and a *Teampull-na-hanait* on the island of Killigray off Harris ? Having got word of this Abbotland or Annait on Loch Rannochside, I searched in the dark pine-wood of Annet, and instead of finding a mere cell I came upon a lost village ! Six or seven ruined houses and a long walled place of graves oriented east and west. In the windless gloom of the wood there was silence. No bird called. No beast or creeping thing appeared. I sat down against the lichened stones, and the smoke of the fire rose like incense in the solitude. A sound of chanting seemed to steal through the unearthly stillness, and the tinkle of God's little bell could almost be heard as the priest in his simple robe spoke the words of mystery to the rude Celts who dwelt about this eerie Annait. Songs of love, the laughter of children, the shout of armed men, the sob of women, and the clash of claymores must often have been heard here. Now—the very trees, all grey with lichen, grow where stood their hearths and altarstone. And when the wind rises it is only to sigh through the dark wood the same ancient coronach of sorrow—" No more, no more, no more returning ! "

At *Craig-an-Odhar*—the dun-coloured rock—there is a strange hatchet-shaped standing-stone on a tree-clad mound by the roadside, which some call the Chieftain's Grave. If he was a local lord he would not have far to travel for his weapons, for at Aulich, a little farther on, there was in olden times a famous smith, said to be in league with the devil, and he made the finest claymores in Rannoch. Rannoch long ago was as famous for its swords as Doune was for its pistols. Deposits of bog-iron were found all round the loch. The Black Wood provided fuel for smelting and charcoal for tempering, and as I write I have before me a piece of iron from the slag smeltings which was picked up at Aulich. Still farther on at Killie-chonan, which is one of the last dwindling crofter communities round these shores, there is an old font lying within the wall of the churchyard. For war and religion have ever been dear to the soul of the Celt.

When you come to the glistening sands of Camus and look across the loch, you will see a little tower on the rocky *Eilean nam Feoileag*—the Isle of Storms. Here some local chief confined a prisoner. Who he was or what his crime I cannot tell. But his friends sent him every year two sacks of apples, and the laird sent out the apples in a boat with two of his ghillies.

" Here are your apples, shifty lad," said they.

" Well, there are more here than I can eat, just men, so take a sack for yourselves," he replied. With that he emptied a whole bagful before the greedy ghillies, who scrambled for them on their hands and knees. But while they were busy at the game of grab, the sly fellow made off in the boat and left them on the island staring after him.

Standing on the Bridge of Gaur at the head of the loch, looking at Rannoch Barracks—once a thatched depôt for the redcoats who were sent to quell those fiery Highlanders, and now an ample lodge—it is part of the old sadness to think that this last lodge on Rannochside, owned by a Robertson, is now changing hands. *Cha till, cha till !* But ere we pass down the south side of the loch, through the glorious Black Wood or old Caledonian forest of Dall, to the last little grave-place at Carie, let us turn aside at Camghouran to an enclosure on a knoll between the road and the loch. This is St Michael's Burial-ground, and it is so full of Camerons that there is scarcely elbow-room for any one else. A fort or a cell once stood on the adjoining hillock. But the legend of St Michael, Camghouran, as I got it, has more murder than religion in it, and with this old tale I make an end of this Rune of Rannoch lore.

There lived a woman of great beauty at Dunan up

STOB A CABER : GLENCOE

the Gaur. A Rannoch Cameron and a Mackintosh of
Moy fell in love with her, but the Cameron was the
lucky one and brought her home to this old fort at
Camghouran. There she bore him seven fine boys.
One day at Perth market the Mackintosh went into
the fletcher's shop to buy a bunch of arrows. He
bought the finest sheaf, and said, " I will fetch the
arrows later on." The Cameron also came to buy
arrows. " I'll take these, for they are your best," said
he. " But they are trysted," said the fletcher. " Who
trysted them ? " " The Mackintosh." " Then I must
have them," and off he went with the arrows. When
the Mackintosh came back and heard the tale, he kissed
the dirk and made off with his men by the shortest
road across the hills for the house of Cameron, who
had twice supplanted him.

He walked in and told the beauty-wife of the
Cameron that she must come with him. But she
flouted him and refused.

" Then," said he, " I will brain every one of these
seven fine boys."

" And if you dared, I would not shed a tear," said
she, thinking he would not dare.

Then he brained six of them on a large stone, but
before he could brain the seventh the beauty-wife
broke down and begged him to spare the boy. He
did that. Just then the Camerons came and slew every
Mackintosh save one, who escaped across the loch by
swimming. But when he reached the other side a
Macgregor cut him down. All the sons of the Cameron
were buried here, and that was the beginning of this
Cameron place of graves at St Michael's, Camghouran.
The stone on which the boys were brained lies to-day
on the left-hand side of the entrance gate, and it is

still called the *Clach-na-Ceann* or Stone of the Heads.
That is the tale as I got it hot from the lips of a Cameron.

" O hearts to the hills of old memory true !
  In the land of your love there are mourners for you ;
  As they wander by peopleless lochside and glen,
  Where the red-deer are feeding o'er homesteads of men.

" For the stillness they feel o'er the wilderness spread
  Is not nature's own silence but that of the dead ;
  E'en the long piping plover and small corrie burn
  Seem sighing for those that will never return."

—J. C. SHAIRP.

XVI

THE BLACK WOOD OF RANNOCH

HAUNT OF THE RED DEER

THE Black Wood of Rannoch is the finest piece of the old Caledonian Forest left in Scotland. It runs for three miles along the south side of Loch Rannoch. Many wide, grassy rides intersect it, from east to west and from north to south, all of it forming part of the fine old estate of Dall. At the time of my last visit the June weather was hot and heavenly, and for eight days I spent every forenoon in the Black Wood. Surely there are few parts of the Highlands more beautiful than this region round Loch Rannoch. From Kinloch Rannoch you look up the whole length of the loch, beyond which lies the desolate moor, to the blue ramparts of the Blackmount and the Glencoe mountains. Looking across from the heights above Dall, your eye rests on Ben Alder and the hills about Loch Ericht and Loch Garry. Despite the intense heat, there were snowfields and patches on the highest hills.

Wandering day after day along the woodland rides, looking and listening, one was aware of the perpetual sense of mystery among the ancient trees which rise out of the long heather and thick blaeberries. The only sound was the husheen of the wind in the tree-tops which gives you the strange feeling that the sea is near.

The Black Wood is haunted by the red deer. They love its sanctuary, and every day you keep watching for the flicker of a brown ear above the undergrowth, where a deer is couched among the heather. At times several deer will move like brown shadows beneath the great trees. If you are going up-wind, you can watch them feeding at leisure ; but, if you are doing down-wind, one sniff of the intruder and away they go with leaps and bounds to some securer sanctuary.

The ground was very dry with the heat, so no new slots—that is, imprints of the deer's hoofs—were found in those odd places where the mud was caked hard. This was unfortunate, for a close observer can, with comparative accuracy, tell from the slots several things—the age of the deer ; whether it was running or walking at the time ; and whether it has passed that way recently or a long time ago. Truly, in the Black Wood you are far from the madding crowd, and in a nature-lover's paradise.

We were too late to see the reddish-brown flowers of the bog myrtle, but flowers were still on the blaeberry clumps, like tiny groupings of bells from the white heather. The Star of Bethlehem, with its six white petals pointed at the tip ; the blue milkwort, showing itself modestly in the grass ; the tiny white bedstraws ; the purple violets ; and the yellow tormentils with their golden petals—they all added to the variety of colour in the carpet of the woods.

Few birds were singing in those hot days ; but the willow warblers, the finches, the little wrens were all there, and an occasional whaup gurled high above the tree-tops. The first thing I noticed in the Black Wood was the great number of moths flitting about. It is, of course, a well-known hunting-ground for entomologists.

RANNOCH : THE BLACK WOOD : VIEW TOWARDS KILCHONAN

Here they come in the season with their treacle-jars and dab the tree trunks with that sweet trap for the unwary lepidoptera. Some of the moths are very rare and beautiful. There used to be a station-master at Struan who was keenly interested in this branch of science, and he kept the collectors informed about the arrival of certain rare specimens.

But, of course, the great trees are the glory of the Black Wood. They are almost all ancient Scots pines, all of them being self-seeded. Is there anything finer in nature than a great pine tree—tall, rugged, strong, and majestic, standing for centuries and defying the storm which roars hoarsely through its branches ? In olden times the trees were often ruthlessly cut down for commercial purposes. When, for example, works for the smelting of iron (or " bloomeries," as they were called) were erected in the seventeenth and eighteenth centuries, at places like Loch Rannoch and Loch Maree, the trees were so ruthlessly cut down that an Act of Parliament was passed on 22nd January 1609 prohibiting the making of iron by using the natural woods of the Highlands for fuel. I have dealt with the history of these " bloomeries " elsewhere. Sufficient is it here to repeat that each furnace used up 120 acres of trees a year to keep it going with carbonised fuel. I have picked up relics of the smeltings at Aulich, on the north side of Loch Rannoch, on the site of one of these " bloomeries."

The vast forests sprang naturally from seeds which had fallen from the woody fruit cones. I had no means of measuring the height of some of the giant trees in the Black Wood, but I measured the girth of several of the largest and found them 10 to 14 feet. The trunk of a Scots pine is very rough, with rugged pieces of red bark separated by deep furrows. The trees yield turpentine and resin in great quantities. You have only to cut a hole in one of the stems and the thick juice which flows will soon harden into clear gum.

Every day my brogues were covered with a golden-green dust, which at first puzzled me. But I soon found out the reason. The stamen flowers grow in dense spikes at the end of last year's bushy twigs, and look like a cluster of yellow grains. In early June these grains send out clouds of fine yellow powder, which floats in the air, settles on the grass and leaves, and accumulates on the shores of the loch, where you can see it lying in little patches. Hence the golden-green dust on the brogues, and the clouds of it floating in the air.

In the olden days, when men knew little about botany, the country people believed that this powder was sulphur which had fallen from the sky after a thunderstorm. On the still hot days the scents in the Black Wood are delicious, resinous, aromatic, and strong.

All along the main rides I noticed cone-shaped heaps of pine needles, each heap like a soft cushion on which one might sit down ; but woe betide anyone who should do so, for each mound is an ant-hill. Break a bit of the surface very gently, and the ants will swarm forth like a regiment of outraged soldiers. This is not the place to give a dissertation on the wonders of ant life, but an ant-hill is the abode of a wonderful community which lives in a palace with innumerable passages, galleries, and rooms. A knowledge of ant life makes one very much inclined to ask : Do ants think ? The following story would seem to show that these remarkable creatures have a highly-developed sense of reason.

A gentleman was sitting at breakfast in Paris one morning when he noticed some black ants busy at the sugar-bowl. He kept driving them away, but they always returned, clambering up the slippery sides of the bowl. Then, to test their ingenuity, he had the bowl suspended from the roof by a string. The ants mounted on each other's backs in a new attempt to get at the sugar. But they failed. Then, after several fruitless attempts they gave it up, and crept away, leaving the experimenter in peace. But before his breakfast was finished he was astonished to see the ants descending the string and dropping into the sugar-bowl one by one. They had scaled the walls, traversed the ceiling, found the string, and so discovered the way into the bowl.

If anyone wishes to know the romance of the ant world, let him read the late Lord Avebury's book on *Ants, Bees, and Wasps.* He was a busy banker and a keen politician, yet one of his experiments entailed watching the visits of one ant to some pupæ in a saucer from 5.55 to 7.6 p.m., noting the behaviour of the ant during 45 visits. She came no more till 8 p.m., and by 10 p.m. she had removed all the pupæ without the help of any other ant. On another occasion Lord Avebury watched from 4.13 a.m. till 7.45 p.m., recording the results of 116 visits of a wasp to some honey. It all amounts to this—that the patience of man is scarcely less of a miracle than the intelligence of an insect.

But to return to the Black Wood. About the beginning of the nineteenth century part of the Black Wood was sold to a Company, and the cutting down of the great trees began. This meant a great deal of work for the natives of the district; but very soon the Company became bankrupt, and the Black Wood was saved.

This Company adopted an ingenious way of conveying the cut timber from the wood to the lochside. Little canals were dug along the hilly part of the wood, with basins for each level. Along these canals the timber was floated. Some way above the loch a sluice was built, and down this water-chute the heavy trees were launched. They descended with great force to the loch. The trees were then bound together in rafts and floated down the loch. It is almost unbelievable, but this old account tells us that they then found their way down the Tummel, which is a very turbulent stream. Then they entered the Tay, which finally bore them to the North Sea. It is even recorded that some of the logs got adrift there and at long last were washed ashore on the coast of Holland.

After some searching I found the remains of one or two of the little canals, which are now very deep ditches; and here and there I found the remains of the basins which must have been the reservoirs for supplying the locks and sluices with water.

I met an old friend who lives at the Black Wood, and who is wise beyond his fellows in the lore of Rannoch and Glenlyon. When speaking of the bankruptcy of the Company, he told me of the primitive system of banking which existed at one time in the remote Highlands. There was usually one man in each district who had accumulated some money and was willing to lend it out at interest. A certain farmer who lived at Culdaremore, on the bank of the River Lyon, was in need of a loan. The moneylender lived at Ardtrasket,

across the river, and he was quite willing to lend.
" Be down at the river to-morrow morning," said he,
" and I will throw the money over to you in a bag."

The farmer was there, and the moneylender from
Ardtrasket came down to his side of the river. He
threw the little bag across, but it fell into deep water
and sank. " Never you mind," said Culdaremore ;
" I was responsible for every penny of it from the
moment it left your hand, and I give you my word of
honour I will repay it." Then the moneylender took
another little bag from his pocket and threw it across
the river. This time it fell on the shingle at the feet of
Culdaremore.

" That is the money," said Ardtrasket ; " the
first bag contained nothing but a stone. I was only
testing your honour. You have given me your word,
and I am satisfied. The money is yours." The Black
Wood can teach us many things. But greater than
them all is this truth of the Gaelic proverb : " A man's
worth is just what his word is worth." Then or now,
that is the soul of all good business.

XVII

THE LAND'S END OF SCOTLAND

DEATH ON DUNAVERTY AND PEACE IN KILCOLMKIL

IT was well called Kintyre, the Head Land, by the old Celtic adventurers, for standing on the top of Dunaverty there is nothing but a waste of waters between you and the dim blue land of Erin. To-day the sunlight is making a shimmer of laughter on the face of the ocean. All the way down the Sound of Kilbrannan the bitter winds blew icy cold from the north-east and whitened every wave with yeasty foam. But now the west wind is blowing beauty over the sea; the green machairland is shining like an emerald carpet; there is a sound of music in the little woods of Keil, where the blackbirds are warbling delicious love-notes; and the heat of the sun draws out the scent of primroses among the graves of Kilcolmkil.

Why did some modern lord of Argyll rename this sunny little world Southend, thus slighting the visionary Celts, who called it by the beautiful name of Muneroi (*moine-ruadh*) or the Red Moss? They seldom erred at a christening, and you have only to turn your eyes inland to see the warm red fields waiting for the brairded corn. The little height of Cnoc Mohr, but one foot short of four hundred, looks down on the kirk and the clachan, the ever-green links and the golden sands. Separating two bays stands the rocky bluff of Dunaverty, where the wintry seas grumble and chafe against its beetling cliff. The scarce recognisable site of its ancient castle can just be traced on the grassy slope of its landward side. Out in the sea, but two miles off, lies the long, low Isle of Sanda, with the smaller Sheep Isle to the east, and the loom of Ailsa Craig against the far-off Ayrshire coast. Beyond the Bay of Carskey to the right the wild headland of the Mull defies the thundering seas, and on the rim of ocean lies that dim blue cloud from which all our ancient blessings of gospel peace and many of our modern tragedies of government have come—Ireland.

Dunaverty dominates the whole landscape. It draws the eye and then the feet to climb its dizzy heights. For, until you know the story of this Rock of Murder, *Dun-a-mortaich*, you have not found the key to the bloodstained fields of Muneroi. Indeed, the whole place is reminiscent of

" Old, unhappy, far-off things,
    And battles long ago."

What Scapa Flow was to the British Navy in the Great War, Sanda out there was to the robbing Danes a thousand years ago. So it was called the Isle of Harbours. The Danish ships rode at anchor under the lee of the island, and a Danish fort once stood on Dunaverty. Here Fergus, the first Dalriadic king from Ulster, landed to reign in Scotland, and some say that Robert the Bruce rested himself on Dunaverty when he was credited with spending all his time over in Rathlin. Long after that, the Macdonalds of the Isles built another castle on the rock, and it was in the strong red Macdonald blood that the greatest tale of Dunaverty was written.

In the hot May days of 1647 the Highland Royalists.

K

under that karry-fisted old rascal, Colkitto Macdonald,
and his son Sir Alastair, were driven down Kintyre by
General Leslie and Argyll with an army of 3000 men.
The Macdonalds tried to check Leslie at Rhunahaorine,
but the cavalry kept driving them on until they had to
fall back on that last hope of the Royalist defence—
Dunaverty, at the Land's End of Scotland. A council
was held somewhere on the sands of Kintyre, and
Archibald Mohr and Archibald Og of Sanda were left
to defend Dunaverty with 200 men. Old Colkitto
sailed with some followers to his castle of Dunniveg,
in Islay, while his son Sir Alastair sailed with the
rest for Ireland, where he hoped to raise an army to
relieve his father in Islay and the two Archibalds on
Dunaverty.

Leslie surrounded the place and sat down for a
siege. The rock was impregnable. Each assault cost
the besiegers dear. It was now sweltering June weather.
The Castle well ran dry. But the garrison was well
supplied with water brought from a distance in pipes
that were secretly led up the rock. Leslie found this
out, cut the pipes, and sat still. As the long summer
days of drought passed slowly by, the Macdonalds were
maddened with thirst. They put out bickers to catch
any rain that might fall. But no rain fell. So, at last,
they had to ask for a parley. Sir James Turner was
sent to make terms, and the desperate prisoners were
allowed to come out of the Castle, but not outside the
defences. For five days the Council held an argie-
bargie about death. Then the bloody work began,
and the 200 prisoners were butchered in cold blood,
or thrown from the cliff to be dashed to pieces on the
rocks. Only one man called M'Coul was spared, and
only one woman, a nurse with a naked babe, escaped—

the man M'Coul was sent to France with a hundred others whom Argyll had smoked out of a cave.

The woman, Flora M'Cambridge, who had been nursing the infant son of Macdonald of Sanda on Dunaverty, fled along the sands carrying the naked child. Campbell of Craignish stopped her, and asked whose child she was carrying. To save the child she said it was her own. "It has the Macdonald eyes," said he, "but no matter—it needs clothing." So the kindly Campbell cut a piece from his plaid and wrapped it round the child. The nurse ran on to a cave near the Mull, and stayed there till the Covenanters had left the district after burning Dunaverty to the ground. The little ghillie grew up to be Ronald Macdonald, the husband of Anne Stewart, sister of the Earl of Bute, and to-day I found the grave of a Ronald Macdonald of Sanda (1681) outside the east end of the kirk at Kilcolmkil!

In yon little oblong enclosure on the links you will find proof of this murder tale to-day. Here are the words carved deep on the stone : "This enclosure was erected by Rev. Douglas Macdonald, twelfth laird of Sanda, in 1846, to mark the spot where his ancestors, Archibald Mohr and Archibald Oig, father and son, were shot and buried after the Battle of Dunaverty, 1647. Other human remains found on the battlefield were also interred here by him." Many bones and some sabre-slashed skulls were found round Dunaverty, and in 1822, after a very high tide, the sand was drifted from a bank at Brunerican, and a great rickle of human bones was found streikit as if in burial. Old days and sad days. The Celt was ever a fighter. Love and war were the passions of his soul. So he went out to battle, and he always fell.

But the Celt is a mystic as well as a man of war.

So leaving the Rock of Murder, we walk round the sandy bay to the old kirkyard of Kilcolmkil, which lies beneath a steep cliff, with its little green graves basking in the sun, by the side of the restless sea.   Here Columba is said to have first set foot on land after being exiled from Erin.   Some modern man of mirth has even carved two footsteps on the rock above the cell, that the credulous may set their feet within them, and dream the readier of Columba of the Waves.   Down there at the back of the ruined church the holy well still flows.   The east end of the building is full of square-cut Norman stones, and two little rounded Norman windows let in the light for the altar.   The church has very plainly been added to at a later date, for it is a long narrow building, 75 feet from east to west, and only 18 feet in breadth, with an unbonded juncture 29 feet from the altar end.   Here, among the grass, within the shadowy wall, and outside in the sun, lie grey recumbent stones, all carved and worn— knights of honour with their swords, priests with their tonsure shears, armorials of MacNeil of Carskey and galleys of Macdonald of Sanda.   And the flowers of Keil !   Primrose tufts so large that you can bury your face in them, pink and white campions, blue hyacinths just bursting, yellow daffodils and wild periwinkles, sheets of white scurvy grass with pale auriculas.   Here at the end of the world is surely an ancient haunt of peace !   Sitting alone among the green graves of Keil, you have only to lift your face to the sun, and the west wind, like some angel invisible, comes sighing over the sea to lay a warm, soft kiss on your cheeks, and drug the senses with a breath of primroses and wild mint.

But to-day this great headland is no longer peopled by the children of the Celts alone.   For after the great slaughter in 1647 came the dread plague of 1665, and the whole of Kintyre was depopulated. As a great white cloud it came over from the mainland, and hung in heavy vapours above the hills. So deadly was the plague that moneys were voted by Parliament for Argyll's relief, and collections were made for the poor folk in the parish churches. Many of the Lowlanders from the mainland—Covenanter folk who had joined the armies of Argyll—were induced to settle in Kintyre with their servants and dependants. The children of these stout Presbyters from Renfrewshire and Ayrshire became siccar seceders, and the result is seen in their barrier of faith to this very day among the graves of Keil. For a little streamlet used to flow from the holy well through the churchyard to the sea, and across that stream the Celts of the older faith and the Lowland Presbyters fought out their battles of conscience while in life. Even to-day you can trace the barrier among the graves ; for at the east end lie all the Highlanders —M'Echans, Lynachans, Camerons, M'Naughts, M'Neils, M'Donalds, M'Millans, M'Ilrevies, M'Phails, Campbells, M'Callums, and M'Cagues ; while at the west end lie all the Lowlanders—Thomsons, Gillons, Reids, Fergusons, Clarks, Montgomeries, Browns, Welshes, Laings, Harveys, Caldwells, Bains, and Ralston of that Ilk. This same Ralston has built himself a tomb enclosed by a stout stone wall, and although all the other graves are oriented, east and west, after the true ritual of the Mother Church, Ralston alone lies looking north, in defiance of all Popish custom, as if in death as in life his dissenting soul still sang : " I to the hills will lift mine eyes ! "

Step along the shore and at the foot of a beetling crag you will come to a huge cave, which measures

96 feet from its mouth to its darkest recess. Here
still camp the children of the wandering man, and in
the winter of 1922 a baby was born in the Smugglers'
Cave. Looking at the dead ashes of old fires and the
litter of straw which cover the floor, we wonder if it
was here that a hundred natives of Kintyre were smoked
out by Argyll and Leslie's men. Like all long-headed
dealers in articles of sale, the old smugglers encouraged
the simple country folk to believe that the cave had
dangerous inland passages, whose black tunnels were
infested by wee folk and ill folk, thus securing privacy
for their illegal trade. This brings us to the legend
of the Piper of Keil.

This piper was a daring carl, for he wagered that
he would put a tune on the chanter and play right
into the black passage, and come out again. So while
his friends watched, the Piper of Keil threw the drones
over his shoulder, blew up the bag and started on his
eerie jaunt, with a little terrier at his heel. At first he
filled the cave with the brave clamour of the Nameless
Tune. Then the piping grew fainter and fainter, until
at last it stopped with an unearthly squeal far ben. An
eldritch laugh followed. Then silence. But the dog
came limping back without any hair on its skin, and
never barked again. And the piper ! He was seen no
more about the sands of Carskey or Keil. But at a
farm five miles inland, those sitting about the kitchen
fire on the wild nights of winter would sometimes hear
beneath the big stone hearth the piper playing the
Nameless Tune, and between the ports they could
hear him wailing wearily this hopeless plaint :

> " I doubt, I doubt
> I'll never win out
> Ochone, for my ageless sorrow."

WEST HARRIS : LOCH TARBERT HOMESTEAD

But the happiest day has an end, and when the sun went down, and the moon sailed high over the silvered sea, we sat in the tower of the Great House of Keil, and listened—not to the sound of the waves—but to that which is stranger than any tale that was ever told. For the House of Keil is now a school for sixty scholars of Argyll. They carry on the traditions of the old Columban monks who once lived in a holy settlement down yonder by the sea. They till the ground, wait upon each other, observe a strict routine of manual labour, and learn the lore of many books, under a scholar superior and a few wise men. Night after night, as we climbed to the tower room, and listened-in to living voices raised in song, to the music of cunning players on strings, and to the converse of many ships at sea—London, Cardiff, Manchester, Birmingham, Newcastle, Glasgow—we linked ourselves up, in this lonely spot, with the laughter and pleasure, the thoughts and happenings of our fellow-men who were hundreds of miles away over the wireless world. Then, when this modern miracle of sound has been silenced, we lay ourselves down to rest, like monks in Muneroi long ago, with the sound of the sea breaking on a midnight shore.

XVIII

THE ISLAND OF MARY ROSE

WHEN Miss Lila Maravan was first playing the part of Mary Rose in Edinburgh, she confessed to an interviewer that she had a great desire to visit the Island of Mary Rose, if only she could find out where it lay. If Sir James Barrie himself were asked, he would probably say, with an innocent smile, that he did not know. But even in the most fantastic Barrie play there is generally a definite foundation for everything—unless when the inevitable Barriesque love for the burlesque runs away with the author and we are treated to a delightful touch of the impossible.

But, where is the Island of Mary Rose? I can only offer a very circumstantial suggestion by relating a few facts, and comparing them with one or two expressions in the play. All that we have to go upon is the speech of Mr Morland when he is telling Simon Blake where the island is. He says that it lies off one of the Hebrides : that he once had a fishing there : that it lay beyond a whaling station : that the island was very near the shore : and that there was a village close by. That is all we get in the play as a clue to the whereabouts of the island.

Some years ago I revisited the Island of Harris and was staying for a short time at Tarbet—that narrow neck of land which separates East Loch Tarbet from West Loch Tarbet. Climbing the barren, rocky hills behind Tarbet, on a clear summer day, a glorious view can be had both east and west—eastward, out of the loch, by the islands of Scotasay and Scalpay, right across the Minch to Hunish Head in Skye and far beyond; westward, straight out to the lone Atlantic, beyond the islands of Soay and Taransay, and by the desolate coast of Harris, where you can trace the road winding along the shore to Amhuinnsuidhe Castle. Here the road proper ends. Some miles out from Tarbet, on this road, there is a whaling station—the only one known to me on the Hebrides. Visitors from Tarbet often walk out to see it. At the time of my last visit to Harris, Sir James Barrie had rented Amhuinn-suidhe Castle for the season, and was resident there for his favourite sport of fishing. The castle stands on the shore of a little sea-loch called Loch Leosavay, which is tucked away in the shelter of low hills, and wonderfully bielded from the Atlantic storms. At the head of this loch, which is only a mile long, stands the village of Leosavay. Opposite the village, and not far from the castle, is a small island in the middle of the loch. Here, in this Isle of Leosavay, I seem to see the Island of Mary Rose, the mystical island that likes to be visited. It is a far cry from the stage of the Haymarket Theatre to little Loch Leosavay and this island, where Sir James, like Simon Blake and Mary Rose and Cameron, must often have taken his lunch while fishing. Is it not most reasonable to suppose that it was here that he dreamed of the fairies and called to life the ethereal conception of Mary Rose ?

So much for the whereabouts of the Island of Mary Rose. But it is much easier to locate in the realms of Celtic superstition the whole foundations of the play.

To begin with, Sir James Barrie has borrowed

more than once his glamorous conception of Eternal Youth from the Gaelic belief in *Tir-nan-Og*, that Land of Heart's Desire where the blessed keep the secret of remaining ever-young and never grow up. As the early Christians spoke of a Land of Promise, so the ancient Celts spoke of a Land of Light, a Land of Ever-living, a Land of Eternal Youth. Sometimes they conceived it as below the depths of the sea ; then they called it a Land under the Waves. Sometimes they thought it was a beautiful Isle of Joy ; then they placed it far out in the magic West on the boundless ocean. Sometimes they associated it with one of those green knolls known to Celtic superstition as *Shians* ; then they called it a place of Fairy Mansions. These abodes of the blessed in *Tir-nan-Og* were peopled by fairy folk ; but a few favoured human beings occasionally reached them, being drawn there during their lifetime ; only—they had to have the inner vision which could see the messenger, and the mystic ear which could hear the call. The Celt has always been sensitive to haunting music, and reference is often made to the ravishing music which was heard in these fairy abodes of the blessed. It lulled to forgetfulness the favoured humans who were invited there. So, this belief in the Land of the Ever-Young has filled the Hebrides with certain fairy mounds and fairy islands from which messengers are sent occasionally to call those who visit them to this land of music and beauty and Eternal Youth.

Sometimes the fairies spirited away a little child, leaving a changeling in its place. Sometimes it was a boy or a girl or even a grown-up man or woman. Was not Mary Rose spirited away for thirty days when she was only a child ? Was she not also spirited away for

ISLE OF MARY ROSE : SOAY MORE

twenty-five years when she was a happy wife and mother ? Tales of this kind could be given from locations all over the Highlands and Islands. One instance will serve.

There is a well-known tale of the " Smith and the Fairies," which was related by the Rev. T. Pattison, in the year 1860, about a smith who lived at Caonisgall, near the parish church of Kilchoman in Islay. The smith's son, like Mary Rose, had been spirited away. So the father, protected by a Bible, a dirk, and a crowing cock, entered the Hill of the Wee Folks, where amid a blaze of lights he found piping and dancing and merriment going on. He struck the dirk into the threshold to keep the door from closing, carried the Bible in his breast as a spell to prevent the fairies from touching him, and demanded that his boy should be restored to him. When the fairies laughed loudly at him, the cock, which had been dozing in the smith's arm, awoke and crowed shrilly. At that, the fairies seized the smith and his son, threw them out of the hill, and the dirk after them, and so the boy was recovered. But, for a year and a day he scarcely spoke. Then, one day he saw his father finishing a sword for a great chief, and suddenly exclaimed, " That is not the way to do it ! " Taking the tools in his hand he proceeded to fashion a sword, the like of which had never been seen before.

Such tales are common in the mythology of many races. Curious music is always heard ; strange calls are heard with the music, offering other-world invitations to come away ; and those who have the hearing ear and are fairy-glamoured are always compelled to go. Here is the foundation, then, in Gaelic myth, of the whole conception of Mary Rose—even to the concealed orchestra, the sound of strange singing, and the elusive call of " Mary Rose !   Mary Rose ! "

Still further, this whole class of stories seems to point to the former existence of a race of men in our islands who were smaller in stature than the Celts, used flint arrow-heads, lived in little conical mounds like the Lapps, knew some mechanical arts, pilfered goods, and stole children. Some of us never go down with painfully bent backs to examine those underground dwellings up and down Scotland, which to-day are called Picts' Houses, but we think of this pigmy race which probably gave rise to the belief in Fairy Folk or Wee Folk. Indeed, Mr John Buchan once wrote a short tale in which he tries to raise the hair of all hill-climbers by suggesting that in a certain lonely part of the Peeblesshire hills, not far from the Scrape, there are still some of those alluring Wee Folk to be met.

But, whether we be pleasure-loving playgoers, or scholarly folk with a turn for seeking the reason behind things, or dreaming mystics with a love of beauty in our souls, Mary Rose will always remind us of those spiritual presences which lurk just behind the veil of this visible world, and her Island that Likes to be Visited will increase the fascination of the Celtic conception of a Land of Eternal Youth.

XIX

THE LURE OF WAYSIDE WELLS

WINTER DREAMS OF SUMMER DAYS

IT is a true saying for some of us that you never really get the best out of summer until you have reached mid-winter. For, when the rain lashes on the window and December storms sweep across the sodden world, then sitting by the cheerful fire with a pipe of peace making blue mist against the gleaming books, a little imagination can bring back summer. Better to be beggared in every circumstance than to live without imagination. For it can keep alive a sense of summer in the soul when winter wearies us with its dark and drip. The burning kiss of sunshine on the cheek, the fragrance of hyacinths in a sun-flecked wood, blue horizons of mountain and sea, a burst of bird-music at dawn, the thousand little pleasures of eye and ear and heart, which a natural man enjoys as he takes his road-side rests and throws another faggot on the fire—these are the imaginings which lighten the darkest days of the year and rob winter of its drear inclemencies.

So in winter-time we delight to call up the memory of many a wayside well. All up and down Scotland there are wells where saints are said to have wrought miracles, where our forefathers worshipped, where lovers and little children brought gifts to appease the spirit of the well. And little wonder. Lie down beside

a spring well in some solitary place and gaze into its
caller deeps. There you will see a little spiral of sand,
perhaps only one grain, being whirled up continually
by some living power unseen. Always moving, spout-
ing, re-forming, and changing, it sends up a new
stream of living water everlastingly. Cold as ice in
summer heat, it defies the frosts of winter and will
not freeze. You can see the green eye of this well far
away on the tawny hillside or on the black-brown moor.
Round its margin grows the greenest grass. Cresses
love to drink at its overflow. Do you wonder that our
ancestors worshipped wells, and laid their little votive
offerings by the side of a spring to propitiate the
mysterious spirit that sent the precious water bubbling
up for bird, and beast, and man ?

But a well never really becomes your own until
you find it yourself. Each has its own story. Only at
one did you first learn the mystery. So when winter
glooms creep over the soul and summer days seem far
away, I have only to shut my eyes and I am there—all
alone, sitting on the little braeface, and drinking water
icy cold.

The first and the last well in the world to me is
on a little moor with a wonderful horizon within
sixteen miles of Holyrood. It lies across a green ravine,
not far from the White Gate and the North Wood,
with an old post stuck into the moor to mark the place.
It is a poor little well as wells go. But the well of home
will always be the most wonderful well in the world,
as King David found out long ago. And this well for
many years was the well of home to me. It still goes
by the name of Jenner's Well, being called after that
namely merchant who for a generation drank its waters
and came here to breathe the finest air in Scotland

when he was weary with business. Here, lying by its
edge, with an eye on its tiny whirling jet of sand, I
first learned the secret of life that is in all wells. To
keep it clean was a periodic pleasure. Here, too, the
children were taught the secret of the well. The oldest
folk in the hills remember it. When we in turn are
too frail to cross the moor, it will be springing still.
Our children's children will be taken to it to hear its
story told. For wells outlast all generations. So I can
see the wee ones of a thousand to-morrows peching up
the green ravine to behold its mystery and slocken their
thirst in the dim days that are yet to be.

What anguish of hearts some wells have seen !
Near the southern end of Loch Oich, in the Great
Glen of Inverness, there is one of the most tragic
wells in Scots history. A monument stands by its
side with seven stone heads carved on its summit, and
this well has been known for generations as *Tobar-nan-
Ceann*, or the Well of the Heads. In the seventeenth
century the Highlands saw many a bloody deed done.
But could any beat this for black treachery ?

The young Chief of Keppoch and his brother had
been sent abroad to the Low Countries for their education, and during their absence the clan affairs and the
estates were managed by their next-of-kin. When the
young Chief and his brother came back a great feast
was held in their honour, and at this very feast the two
lads were murdered in cold blood by their jealous
relatives. The bard of the clan—Ian Lom or John the
Bare—was roused to dreadful eloquence, and he sent
his verses of fire broadcast to every castle in the countryside. Himself of the family of Keppoch, it was Ian
Lom who guided the great Montrose across the snows
of Corryarrick, and sang the triumph of his clan at

Inverlochy, where the Campbells were cut down like standing corn. The Government at last took action, and authorised Macdonald of Sleat to punish the murderers. John the Bare guided him into Lochaber, where they found the guilty seven in bed. They dragged them out, cut off their heads, packed them in a creel, set the creel on a man's back, and by dawn were at the gates of Glengarry. But before presenting the seven heads to Macdonell of Glengarry they washed them in this well, and the well to this day is called the Well of the Seven Heads. To make no mistake with posterity, a monument was erected, which tells the tale in Gaelic, Latin, French, and English, that every gangrel of the road to all time might know this act of treachery and the summary justice which followed it. It may be the freit of a foolish man, but to me the water of that well will always taste brackish and wersh.

One of the finest ploys for a wandering Scot is to trace a river from the sea to its source. The Tay is our longest river, being 117 miles in length from its source to the sea. But of the tens of thousands who know Dundee how many have traced the lordly Tay to its mysterious well-head ? The Tay is a river of many names. Up the first stretch of its broad-bosomed waterway it is just 31 miles to Perth ; another 31 of splendid salmon reached from Perth to Tummel ; 15½ more to Kenmore ; a fine 14½-mile sail up Loch Tay to Killin ; and then in its last 25 miles it becomes the Dochart to Loch Dochart, the Fillan to Coninish, and the Coninish to Ben Lui.

Well do I remember the day when I first sought the source of the Tay on Ben Lui. The rain and mist never ceased, unless for those little, tantalising intervals of lifting cloud which make a day of Highland rain all

the more hopeless. The Coninish riverside is not an
esplanade, nor is the north face of Ben Lui a gentle
incline. But up and up through the rain and mist the
way led. The streams were big that day. But the
steeper the smaller, and at last, in a corrie wellnigh
3000 feet up, behold a gush of caller water coming
from beneath the rocks of Ben Lui ! That is the source
of this many-titled river, the longest and greatest—
although not the best—of our Scots streams. For the
best is farther south !

But the wells of the world are not all Wells of
Wearie. Scotland is full of Wells of Love ; and every
well of love is a wishing well. To close the eyes by the
winter fire and go over the wishing wells we have
visited is like taking a pilgrimage of high romance,
and not always alone. The one I like best is a wishing
well in Glen Lyon. It is an iron-tasted spring by the
roadside, with a shelf of stone fitted above it and a
bank of grass on the top. The dark recess of the stone
shelf is generally filled with little stones. Every one of
them means a wish expressed by a passer-by—some
weary old body who still sees visions ; some douce
mistress or man who never places a stone there without
making sure that no one is looking ; or some happy
lover and his lass who stop and go through the dear
old play with hope in the heart, laughter on the lips,
and maybe a kiss to make siccar. Never have I seen
that ledge empty of stones. Never am I ashamed to
place one there. For we are all sweir to let go the
old romantics of life, and these stones to-day at the
wishing well link up the most orthodox Christian
with his pagan ancestor who worshipped the god of
the well.

The next well tells the same story. It is the Cheese

Well on Minchmoor, that Border upland where the old post road crossed from Yarrow to Tweedside. Very pleasant is the walk up this ancient road from Traquair past the Warlock Knowes, the Louping-on-Stane, and the Clattering Path to the Cheese Well. Here the auld-farrant travellers used to drop little bits of cheese as votive offerings to the fairies who haunted this mountain path. Did not the lad come this way from Yarrow to see his lass at the scrunts o' birk downby? And could he fail to bring her back this way one day—not on a Scots convoy, which always means parting at the long last—but on their wedding jaunt to his home in Yarrow? I like to sit here and think of her on the pillion as she rides past this Cheese Well, a blushing bride, with no more fear of Warlocks when she goes by the Knowes and her horse's shoes making sparks on the clattering path.

> " They were blest beyond compare
> When they held their trysting there,
> Amang thae greenest hills shone on by the sun."

The great Montrose! He, too, clattered past the Cheese Well on his flight from fatal Philiphaugh, never drawing rein until he came to the house of Traquair. There he knocked at an old friend's door. But the traitor Traquair shut the door on his face. He was not at home. He had seen the cat jumping before Philiphaugh. So he changed his coat and now reserved his welcome for Leslie, Argyll, and Lothian, who soon arrived in pursuit of the great Marquis. So we turn away from this Jacobite turncoat and remember Walter Scott and Mungo Park at the Cheese Well. When they parted over yonder on Williamshope Ridge,

Sir Walter described the good-bye thus : " I stood and looked back—but he did not." There you have strong friendship, for these were a pair of real men.

My last well of dream is the greatest and in some ways the most wonderful of all. It is not remote, for it stands at the foot of a side-path in the village of Portmoak, the capital of that quaintest of all the shires in Scotland—the Bishopshire. A sleepy place is Portmoak on a summer afternoon when the old folks are dovering in their chairs and the pigeons are preening themselves on the step-gables. It has old-world houses, a sough of Seceding history in the name of Erskine, with the Bishop's Hill and the Bishop's Moss not far away. Long ago the lands of Portmoak belonging to the Church formed a separate regality under the Bishop of St Andrews. So it was called the Bishop's Shire. But even yet, those who love these sequestered villages at the foot of the Bishop's Hill—Portmoak, Kinnesswood, and the two Balgedies—speak of the Bishopshire as they tramp along Loch Leven side.

But to me the miracle of the Bishopshire is Scotland Well. It is a great square parapeted stone cistern with a slated roof above, wooden pillars, and open sides. Down in that square tank the water is always bubbling up from beneath the yellow sand, not in little spirals but in great eruptions like a boiling bath. When the Romans were in Scotland they must have looked with wonder on this well. Long before that, the heathen Picts and Scots would worship at its side. Ever since this world of Scotland began, it has been bubbling up in never-ending commotion. I have seen it in summer-time, in the freezing days of spring, at the blazing hour of noontide, and in the blue dusk of twilight. I like it best in that eerie gloaming hour, when the stars are coming out in the frosty sky and the lamps are being lit in the little kitchens of the Bishopshire. Then, leaning over the stone parapet, all alone, I listen in the gloom to the ghostly sound of the bubbling water and the even rush of the overflow. It is a haunted place with a timeless mystery all its own.

XX

WANDERING WILLIES

MEMORIES OF THE ROAD

To the real lover of the road every summer brings its own adventures in friendship, and every winter its memories of many a tramp acquaintance. Most people keep to their own class, and live without much knowledge of those who move in the other classes of society. But the wandering man knows no class. He is the true democrat. He takes the world for his pillow, and becomes the friend of all humanity. When winter comes the children of the wandering man return to the towns and cities and lose themselves in the crowd. No more the call of the birds at dawn, and the long white ribbon of road stretching across the moorland under a blazing sun. No more the noontide rest by the river, or the evensong of blackbirds and thrushes in the gloaming. Instead of the witching nights of June, which were but lambent twilights lit by a few pale stars, come the pitchy glooms of December and January, the splash of rain or the rattle of hail on the window, and all the miseries of winter inclemency. There is nothing for it then but to draw the curtains, wheel an arm-chair to the fire, and watch the flames making giddy ghosts along the book-lined walls. In that happy hour memory calls up, one by one, those companions of the road who filled the summer days of travel with many a glad surprise.

I met Red River when July brought us the only handful of sweltering days last summer. The fishing on the loch was reduced to one big trout a day, with a few exciting nibbles. To a man who wears the seven-leagued boots, and has a lust of wandering in his heart, eight hours in a fishing cobble under a blazing sun, when the hills are a dream of celestial beauty, and the wild flowers grow prodigal on the bank of every burn, spells little else than prison. But the company was of the best, and Red River was the rare one for telling a tale. His soul was as Gaelic as his tongue, but in his wandering life he had spent some years on a Red River settlement in the Far West, and so had earned his name for a far-travelled fellow. He is of the order of man who never grows old even when he is elderly, with an eagle nose on a keen face, and an eye as clear as a gled's. Lythe as a withy, skilled in every art of piscatorship and hillcraft, Red River would make a sportsman's orraman *de luxe*.

Nor did he deliberately avoid the pleasures of this life, for he told me that a funeral down Tummelside was a cheerier affair than a wedding up in Rannoch. We rowed the loch from end to end the livelong day, and the beauty of the world was wonderful. But, in spite of Red River's lures, the fish would not take. So, on the second day I took something heavier than a fishing-rod under my oxter, and tried the effect of putting a tune on her. I was told it was not the usual way to fish, but at least the music brought one ugly pike on board. When the time to eat and drink came round, we landed at the head of the loch, where the sand gleams golden. Red River wandered off politely by himself to a distant spit of sand, where the tireless soul began to fish for eels. After a time I joined him and put a strathspey called " Highland Whisky " on the pipes. With that the swanky man was footing it like a young one, on the sand. When we had blown ourselves into a pother of heat we sat down on the gunwale of the boat. It was then, when the blue smoke was curling up in little rings, and our heads were close together, and there was not a breath of wind to carry our secret, that we compared notes on the scandalous methods which some men employ in taking fish or rabbits or birds or deer without a sound. Izaak Walton at that moment would not have called us orthodox. The rare adaptabilities of fine wire ; the wee bit elastic and the forked stick ; the splash net in the small hours at a burn-mouth ; the gaff with a blacksmith's mistake on the crook of it ; Neptune's own trident ; the burning torch ; the naked hand, or the fingers that know how to tickle under water—these are commonplaces of the wilds. There were others, but they are of no interest to the general public. One, however, was new to me—a sure way to snare a deer, neck high, on its own tracks, in dead silence, within a wood. But, like the secret of the man who killed the Red Fox, that story would be spoiled in the telling. The only thing certain is, that Red River had no experience of the methods discussed ! But—who that loves the wild life of the river, the woodland, or the hills, can doubt that in the heart of every natural man there is this lust for the risky sport, which some would call by a less euphonious name ? O Red River ! I have only to shut my eyes in the dreary winter months within this room, which is far removed from all the tricks of the chase, legal or otherwise, and I can see you dancing in the sunshine on yon spit of sand.

Later in the summer I met quite a different type of

man. I saw him first at a farm steading, and often
after that on the Perthshire roads. He had plainly the
stamp of the town on him, and wore spectacles when
he was at work. A cast of trout flies adorned the old
hat which was set jauntily on the grey head of this
clever-faced old man, and a little leather bag was slung
over his shoulder. He lived in town all winter, and
only took to the road for the summer months. He was
a mender of clocks and watches, and therefore a skilly
man with his fingers. He had travelled Scotland from
Loch Naver to the Tay, and in his younger days had
been a pearl-fisher—an industry which is rapidly dying
out because the mussel beds in our Scots rivers are
being rapidly destroyed. You can still see an odd
tinker or wandering fellow fishing from his little boat
in the Tay or in a pool on the Lyon, when the water is
low, using his pearl-fisher's glass, which is, for all the
world, like a great speaking-trumpet with a sheet of glass
fixed on to the bell-mouth end. When this is thrust
down into the still water the pearl-bearing mussel can
easily be seen in the bed of the stream. Once, in a deep
pool of the Tay, I saw the pearl-fisher's glass used to
locate the body of a drowned priest, so clearly can
objects on the floor of a deep pool be thus discerned.

From the old pearl-fisher I learned many things,
for " a gaun fit's aye gettin'." The Ythan and Ugie in
Aberdeenshire were for a long time the finest pearl-
producing rivers in Scotland. It is told that in the
good old days before the Union, when a pound Scots
had only the value of one shilling and eightpence, or
one-twelfth part of the pound sterling, an Aberdeen
merchant offered a fine set of Scots pearls from the
Ythan, to a London dealer for £100, meaning, of course,
pounds Scots. The jeweller promptly offered £80,

but the Aberdonian declined it as he had himself paid £80 (Scots) to the Ythan pearl-fishermen. The pearls were very good, so the London jeweller laid out the £100 in English money on the counter. Aberdonians are not given to showing their feelings when awkward circumstances arise, so the Aberdeen merchant quietly pocketed the money and went home to set up a new standard for the price of Scots pearls in the London market.

Many small pearls are still found in Scots rivers, but the finds are very uncertain, and only mussels gathered off shingly beds yield pearls of any value. A large Scots pearl is still a thing of beauty.

I often wonder where the asthmatic old pearl-fisher is passing the gloomy winter days, oiling the wheels and mending the springs of old watches and clocks!

A very different character was the seller of tapes and pins and brooches; and yet she too is a bit of life. I met her one fine windy day on a road beloved of Robert Louis Stevenson, where there is a deep dip in the woodland path to a bridge, and a steep hill on the other side. She was very old, very feeble, and very dirty. A big basket contained all her belongings— laces, tapes, safety-pins on cards, a pickle tea and sugar, a packet of candles, and an assortment of brass gewgaws with coloured glass jewels in them for the simple milk-maids at the farms. Coming up behind her, I saw it was all she could do to carry her basket in the teeth of the wind. A taint of whisky was in the breeze. She was very talkative and sore forfochen. So I took the basket, and we made for the brae together.

Did ever anyone see a sorrier wreck of woman-hood, and yet she kept babbling of her bonny girlhood!

She was seventy-five. Her grey hair was all matted.
The toothless, besotted face had been bitten by rats
as she lay out at nights in barns and sheds. A gin
bottle lay in the basket. A pair of happy lovers passed
us on the hill with a blank stare, as if it was an ill thing
to help an old done limmer who was toshie. When
we got to the level road again we parted, and I bought
a paper of pins at a price which would have earned the
contempt of the Aberdeen pearl-dealer. But for all
her rags and wounds and gin, old Jean was a bit of
God's own clay which had been sorely mishandled.

> " ' Shall He that made the vessel in pure Love
>   And Fancy, in an after Rage destroy ? '
>   None answered this ; but, after Silence, spake
>   A Vessel of a more ungainly Make :
>   ' They sneer at me for leaning all awry ;
>   What ! did the Hand, then, of the Potter shake ? ' ' "

There are great contrasts on the road. I am thinking now of the apple-faced old man—small, stout,
well-groomed, with a rosy, clean-shaven face, a pair
of twinkling eyes, and that uplifting smile which,
through long habit, had fixed a look of cheery optimism
on the old fellow's face. He was eighty-five, had been
a coachman in the far-off city for fifty years, and was
now returning to his native clachan on the loch-side to
spend his last days among his old friends—most of
them, alas ! beneath the sod of the old kirkyard.

" You're making for Achnamara ? "

" Yes, I am that. I was born there."

" Then you'll be either a Cameron or a Macgregor ? "

" A Cameron, and one of the last of them."

He was good to look at in the sunset, with the after-
glow shining on his red, round, apple-like cheeks.

To come home again at eighty-five with the heart of youth and the light of heaven shining on the face—this is surely the triumph of life.

There are men of every condition and rank tramping the roads of Scotland to-day. Ask me not for their story. My only ploy is to give them a cry in the passing, to offer a light to them, and to greet them one and all as brothers.

I might tell of many more acquaintances made on the friendly road, but these samples of one summer must suffice. We cannot solve each other's problems. The only thing to do is to trudge on cheerily, to despise no one, and to make the best even of the worst. So, many a time, after parting from one of these Wandering Willies, I have sat down, a trifle sadly, at the foot of a hedge, and, taking out the little pipe, have sent the notes of their own tune dribbling down the breeze :

" Home no more home to me, whither must I wander,
  Hunger my driver, I go where I must ;
Cold blows the winter wind over hill and heather,
  Thick drives the rain, and my roof is in the dust.

" Fair the day shine as it shone on my childhood,
  Fair shine the day on the house with open door ;
Birds come and cry there, and twitter in the chimney,
  But I go for ever, and come again no more."
                                        —R. L. Stevenson,

XXI

WINTER BEAUTY

FIRES OF DEATH AMONG THE HILLS

STONY streets and huddled houses; long, barrack-like West-end crescents, where every man puts a key into a door which is exactly like a thousand other doors; slum tenements that are high almost to giddiness, where thousands live like rabbits in an over-crowded warren, but without a whiff of clean earth-scented air at their doors; gutters running full of foul scourings; crowds of weary-faced men and women battling with the problems of a too unsimple civilisation—when we look at it all from the standpoint of a natural man, it seems like an elaborate prison-house into which man has locked himself.

But the primitive instincts after the music and colour of nature leap out from us in the most unexpected ways. A very little thing will do it. Then we grow restless and unhappy in our stone houses and hot rooms. A birch-tree opposite my window did it for me—a town-imprisoned birth with its thousand golden shekels shivering in the sun. It multiplied its beauty day by day until I saw the great open spaces among the hills, by the rivers, and in the woods, literally blazing with gold. Then, like a lover who cannot keep away from his beloved, but is always ettling after another look at her face and another song from her lips before the long farewell, I stole three days and ran away.

It was ridiculous. The day was the dullest possible. The rain lashed down persistent. Glasgow, as we passed through, was a perfect cauldron of unclean mists and smoke. The Clyde lashed its shores above Dumbarton with waves of drumly mud. Pitchy darkness and driving rain obliterated all the beauties of loch and river and mountain as we sped northward into the night. But hope sang songs in the heart all the way, and in the very centre of the waste places of the bens and glens a face was often thrust out of the window into the dripping gloom with a certain knowledge that here, and there, and yonder, were old haunts and unseen beauties lying among the hills. At a nameless little station below a corrie the train stopped. Two strong hands met in the glare of the lamps. Rain ran down the face of a buirdly form that stood smiling on the platform. There was a cheery word about the record 42-lb. fish caught in a pool down by. The roar of the salmon river in the glen was like music, after the train had crept away along the hillside into the night, like a fiery snake making for the great moor. The rain had been lashing for weeks, but they told me it would be better weather to-morrow now that the lucky one had come. So down the steep black brae we plunged. Then a lighted window, the cosiest fire in Scotland, a steaming meal delicious beyond words, the heartsome lilt of a Gaelic voice which two men at least have long since learnt to obey, and the hundred thousand miles of weariness had been put between the cobble streets and the solitudes of a great wilderness.

Next morning beauty came like a sunburst of good-luck. The rain was over. Mist was trailing from the high tops. The sun came out, not suddenly, but fitfully, feeling its way through the rain clouds, until it had gained some noontide courage. The music and the colour were all there. The whole earth was on fire. The wonder of the November world filled the soul with a reverent awe. If only the tens of thousands of city dwellers who race through the Highlands after pleasure in summer could spare a day and bring an eye to look upon these waste places of Scotland now, what a revelation it would be! There is no colour in the whole year like the colour of late October or early November in the North. It is so wonderful that it is both the despair and joy of an artist to paint it or a writer to describe it.

These great hills which were so green last July are now one mass of ruddy browns and burning reds. Not one green blade of grass, not one patch of purple heather, but everywhere you look, red and brown, russet and gold. The colour of the mountain grasses is indescribable. Down in the Lothians November still shows bright green fields between the early furrows of brown. But here, in the centre of a great deer forest, the tall, coarse hillside grasses are all tawny and brown, like a lion's mane.

In the woods alone you will find some evergreens. But even there, the infinite variety of colour is but the infinite variety of flame. For the woods are on fire— burning to their death in great glory. The sombre green of the pines alone is everlasting. But the golden tassels of the birches, the tawny cones of the larch-trees, the red patches of the rowans—they are all caught in the splendid fires of death. How the colours of the red hills and these flaming woods are intensified when the level rays of the November sun break through the clouds in the late afternoon and send a tongue of intenser fire along the bens and glens and woodlands !

The loch was higher than I have ever seen it. So much rain has fallen this season. But it was well worth while one morning to bail the boat and row the two or three miles to the top. The showers were over, the wind came away fresh, there were soft fleecy white clouds hanging in the liquid blue of the November sky, and the sun poured down on the rippling water, making it one great sheet of sapphire set in a surround of red and gold. At the top of the loch the high water had covered the sands which usually stretch wide and golden in summer-time. Even the rough road which leads to the old Castle was under water here, and the walk was sodden and soppy. But the very water-pools and mossy dubs shone with a dull beauty among the burning moors, and the wall-encircled graves of the Fletchers were kissed by the fitful sun.

Only once, as I wandered along the road from Doire Darrach to the bridge, did I see a spot of emerald. At a turn of the road it blazed like green fire among the heather. The sun was very low. Looking into the level beams, I saw a grey rock covered with moss. Seen against the sun, the moss was the only spot of vivid green in the landscape. But, when I passed the stone and looked back at it in the full light of the sun, the brilliant colour was all gone. I retraced my steps again, and faced the level rays. There it was once more, a little green fire, blazing brilliantly on the top of the grey boulder, as vivid as ever. So much can be seen or missed in nature on the instant !

Then, the clouds gathered, and a sudden squall of rain swept down the Glen. The great legs of the sun straddled through the rain-cloud like two shafts of a searchlight—one seeking out the secrets of Ben Dorain, the other focussed on the slopes of Ben Veigh, two little moving spots of light. When the rain was past the sun shone out again, and a great rainbow made evening glory across the whole forest, with its one foot on Clashgour and the other on Barravurich. That was the last gleam of beauty. The twilight fell, sudden and solemn. A wedge of wild duck flew across the wan waters of the loch. A great heron rose lazily from the sedges. In the darkening night a stag bellowed a challenge somewhere up the hillside as he wandered jealous among his hinds. Yonder was the light in the window. Here was the keystone of the old bridge. So standing by the parapet above the rushing water, with the loom of the everlasting hills making black the night, I said good-bye.

XXII

A KING OF THE ROAD

THE LAST OF THE MINSTRELS

I saw him first near a glen-foot that lies on the wise man's side of Schiehallion, but I was taigled at the time with respectable company, and could not get near him for a confab. I noted his direction, however, and the extraordinary slowness of his progress, so I was able to overhaul him next day within a mile of the old farm. In all my wanderings I never hope to meet in with another such.

What was he like ? A lost laird or a king of men gone astray. In his young days he must have been six feet four in his bare feet. But now he was eighty years old, and had travelled a weary way since he had put love over the lass that turned her back on his infirmity. A big, buirdly man still, he wore a blue Kilmarnock bonnet, innocent of ribbons, cocked jauntily on a head of curly white hair. A face that was still handsome by ordinary, but weatherbeaten to a dull brick-brown, with an eagle nose and a white moustache that covered a mouth which had a hint of weakness in it, a middling chin and blue eyes, with a far-away look in them that gave him the appearance of a man who has visions. Vision indeed was his only sight, for—he was blind !

And the clothes ! A red tartan kilt of the clan that

needs no apology in Lochaber, above a pair of sun-burnt leathery knees ; black and red marled hose, and great boots like shoes of fortune, with a heavenward tilt about the toes. Over all he wore an old Highland cloak that had still a hint of the fine gentleman in its cut, and slung across the shoulders on a leathern strap were two pokes, which doubtless contained the treasures of the humble, with a fiddle-case dangling on his breast.

In spite of the blind eyes he carried his head high, for he held in his left hand the chain of a dour-looking collie that led him, and in his right hand he carried a stout stick, with which he kept tapping the road in front of him. A second collie trotted by his side or ranged in front like a touchy scout defiant. Here, by my certie, was a namely king of the road.

A growl from the collie made the first advance dangerous, but soon we got into step, and the travel-talk began. My own duds were little better than his, for it had been a long, tearing day among the rocks. Yet, blind as he was, he jaloused by the voice what I was.

" Parson or dominie ? "

" The first.   But how did you guess ? "

" Because ye speak like one that explains."

" Have you the gift, then ? "

" Well—I am old and done now, and when the body fails the thrum of the spirit is easy broke."

He knew Scotland from the wilds of Aberdeen to the homely Lothians. He had something to say, I remember, of the old Kirk of Linlithgow, where James IV. saw the freit of a blue-gowned bogle that warned him to keep away from Flodden, and then vanished.

With that we came to the old farm.

" Come in and eat."

" No ; I never enter a house."

" Then out here on the grass."

So we sat down side by side, a pair of Dusty Dans, and the wise one brought out the tea.

It was a queer meal. He produced a wooden cogie from some secret place beneath the cloak and drank his tea from it, taking sip about with the collies. When he ate a bap or a cake, the dogs ate from it at the same time, so that the three mouths kept nibbling at it together. The slightest attempt to touch a dog or any of his belongings brought a snarl and a snap.

" Dinna meddle the doggies, or they'll fly at ye and worry ye."

They were his only friends, and his jealous keepers. He lived with them, ate with them, slept with them—inseparable.

Then came more talk about the hills, the mist, the silence, and the lonesomeness. He was a great hand at the ancient prophecies in the Book, and talked like one who was far-ben in the mysteries. He put the truth in this never-to-be-forgotten word—

" Ye can never win close to Him till ye climb high up into the mists, all your lone, where there is never another to break the thrum."

He told me what was to be and what had been with myself, sitting there with the great hills about us, and the river whispering at our feet. Even the wise one had to admit his uncanny knowledge, and I was sweir to let him go. But before he took the road I ettled after his domicile, and this is all he said :—

" When you think o' me in yon dark town, call me the Man who wears the Urim and the Thummim ! "

With that we parted at the keystone of the bridge

that crosses the spatey river, and to this day I can hear the eerie tap-tap of the blind man's stick on the camber of the hollow arch as he moved slowly away with the dogs trotting by his side.

Beannachd! If only we could learn each other's story there would be no need of novels. But the patient one will often unravel the tangled skein. I never saw the blind gangrel again ; but years after, when he was dead, I got his whole story in a Highland kitchen.

It began with a bald notice which appeared in a public print :—

" Notice is hereby given, that the estate of John Macgregor, known as 'The Blind Fiddler,' a vagrant of Forfarshire, who died in Kirriemuir Almshouse on 27th December 1916, has fallen to His Majesty as *ultima hæres.*"

Then the details of the story leaked out one by one.

There was nothing of the usual tramp about John Macgregor, who for fifty years travelled the highways and byways of Scotland. Rather was he the last of the old minstrels. Born somewhere north of the Cairnwell, he was a kenspeckle man about Braemar, Invermark, Glenshee, Strathardle, and Dunkeld, although I met him farther west than that. A teller of many tales, he knew the Book from end to end, and the inward eye saw all the more because blindness threw him back on the secrets of the soul. Why had such as he taken to the life of a wandering fiddler ?

The story goes that when he was an upstanding lad of great strength and beauty, with a lover who was all his own, he was working in a quarry, when a blast went off and blinded the young giant for life. To the cream of womanhood a blind man is a man doubly dear. But to this Aberdeenshire queyn the blind man was a spoiled man. So she turned her back on his sorrow and consoled herself with some other loon. But the blinded giant was a proud Highlander. Suffering in silence, he said nothing. Then, when he was well enough, he slipped away and took the old road that leads to nowhere.

After that he fiddled his way through life, as many another slighted one has done. Often in a barn he made the rafters dirl with the clamour of the reel, when the country lads and lasses kept the kirn going to the skreich of day with hoochings and laughter. Yet his tunes were not all gay. At times the fiddle would wail out some low broken-hearted melody that came from the deeps of his own soul—the slow, sad memories crowding on each other like tears from a lover's eyes. When he played to himself it was as if he was eternally seeking some comfort which he could never find. But none could get his story by simply plucking his sleeve. He fiddled for the gentrice and he fiddled for the canalyie. He once fiddled before Queen Victoria on Deeside. His public tunes were always cheery. But his best tunes were his lonely tunes, and they were always sad with remembering.

He slept under the stars for choice. A fine bed in summer-time, when in the warm nights of August the purple heather drugs the sleep of a weary man with honey-scented dreams, and the grouse cock awakes him at dawn for a sun-splashed bath in the tumbling torrent. But a hard bed in winter-time, when the wind drives the rain in pitiless sheets down the glens or the silent falling snow makes sleep a thing near to death itself.

" But for the doggies," he once said, " I wadna be here this day. Often when I'm far frae shelter

I dig a hole in the snow and lie down in my cloak, and the doggies snuggle round my neck. The snow covers us up, but we dinna mind, for the three o' us are cosy and warm thegither."

But it came to the last sleep with John Macgregor at the hinder end. One bitterly frosty night in December this old king of the road lay down to sleep on the road-side near Greenmyre Farm, in the parish of Kingoldrum. His fiddle was broken. He had played his last tune. His dogs were dead. No warm paws were about his neck. He was all alone under his favourite stars. Next day a kindly farmer found him unconscious, and by the mercy of Heaven he never regained his senses to realise where he lay. It was all as he would have wished it to be—the open road, the frosty silence, the glittering sky, with no one near to break the thrum. They found £50 on him. So his wee strip of earth was his own to the last, and the rest of his simple hoard went to the King, whose grandmother had once listened to his music.

Every man's story is his own by right. When it comes to the end of all things, none can tell with surety the dreams that trouble a man's last sleep. But were I to guess the secret of John Macgregor's wandering life, I would set my venture down in these immortal words :—

> " Had we never loved sae kindly,
> Had we never loved sae blindly,
> Never met and never parted,
> We had ne'er been broken-hearted."

GLOSSARY

Argie-bargie, dispute, contention

Beannachd, Blessing ! Benediction !
Beeking, basking
Bield, shelter
Biere or *bere*, barley
Bodach, an old man
Buirdly, large, well-made
Byke, a nest or hive of bees

Cailleach, an old woman
Caller, fresh
Canalyie, the common people, rabble. (Fr. *canaille*)
Cateran, a highland robber
Ceilidh, gossiping, story-telling
Certie, troth ; *by my certie !* take my word for it
Clachan, a small group of houses
Clanjamfrey, company, mob
Cloverstones, stones gathered off a cloverfield
Cogie, small wooden bowl
Confab, conversation
Coronach, a funeral dirge
Creach, a foray, or expedition to drive off stolen cattle. (Gaelic)

Dirl, a tremulous stroke, vibration
Dool, sorrow
Dooms, very, absolutely
Douce, sedate, sober
Dover, to snooze
Drones, the three large, upright, wooden pipes attached to the bagpipe and thrown over the left shoulder
Dwam, a swoon or dream

Ettling, aspiring, attempting, striving after

Ferlie, a wonder
Forby, besides, over and above
Forfochen, exhausted, fatigued
Fornent, opposite to
Freit, a superstitious notion

Gangrel, a vagrant
Garron, a small horse
Gaun, going. Sc. proverb, " A gaun fit's aye gettin' "=a fellow whose foot is always on the road is always getting something
Gey, considerable
Gillean-Dhe, Friend of God, *e.g.* Culdee. (Gaelic)
Gled, a kite, a hawk
Guddle, to catch fish with the hands
Gurly, bleak, stormy

Howes, used both for a hollow and a mound

Jaloused, guessed

Karry-fisted, left-handed
Keening, lamenting
Kenspeckle, prominent, easily noticed
Kent, known
Kirn, the feast of harvest home
Kist, a chest or box

Limmer, a scoundrel
Lown, calm, sheltered

Machar (*machair*), a green plain by the shore

'Nainsel', himself
Namely, famous

Orraman, man employed to do odd jobs

Ower, over

Oxter, armpit

Papingo, the popinjay, or mark like a parrot, set on a pole to be shot at by archers in olden time

Peching, panting, breathing hard

Queyn, queen, a young woman

Reiving, robbing

Sacring, consecration (sacring bell)

Scrunts, scrubby trees or bushes

Shouchet, shovelled in hastily

Sib, related to

Siccar, sure, certain

Siller, money

Skreich, a shrill cry. " Skreich o' day " refers to the cock's shrill crowing at dawn

Slocken, to slake the thirst

Smooring, stifling, smothering, damping down a fire : also used of drifting snow

Soo-backit, like the back of a sow

Splairging, splashing

Spurtle, a wooden stick to stir broth or porridge

Steep the withie, to steep or soak withies (willow wands) in water, bend them, and nail them to a closed door is the sign that the householder has left home suddenly

Stey, steep

Stravaiger, a wandering, strolling fellow

Streikit, to extend, lay out (a dead body)

Sweir, slow, reluctant

Taigle, to detain, delay

Tearlach Og, Young Charlie, *i.e.* Charles Edward Stewart. (Gaelic)

Thole, to bear, to suffer

Threeped, contended, to urge insistently

Thrum, the loose end of a weaver's yarn

Tirl, to thrill ; a smart stroke —also " to tirl at the pin "— twisting and rasping with the ring on the risp or iron pin of an old door

Tosh, toshie, tipsy

Tulzie, a fight, scrap, brawl

Wersh, unpleasantly tasteless, so unsalted as to be positively distasteful

Whaup, curlew

Whiles, at times

Win, manage (win thro'=to get through)

Withie, a flexible twig or willow wand

PRINTED IN GREAT BRITAIN BY OLIVER AND BOYD LTD., EDINBURGH

SCOTTISH PILGRIMAGE IN THE LAND OF LOST CONTENT

By Rev. Dr T. RATCLIFFE BARNETT

CONTENTS

With 24 full-page illustrations from photographs by Robert M. Adam.
Crown 8vo. Cloth. Pp. xiv + 208 Published price **6/-** net

Press Reviews

Alike in the topographical and biographical senses his new book has a wide range. . . . Dr Barnett's deep interest in the antiquities of the regions of which he writes carries with it no hint of dull pedantry, for his motive is his preoccupation with the human background. This admirably written and well-illustrated book takes a worthy place beside *Border Byways* and *The Land of Lorne.—The Scotsman.*

Up and down the country Dr Barnett rambles—Galloway, the Lammermoors, Cromarty, Lismore are but a few of the places—talking of these and similar matters ; and his twenty-six short sketches are shot through with nostalgia of quite agreeable variety. They reflect the author's affectionate longing for times gone by, and they will stir the work-bound reader to an equally ardent longing to be walking once more in Scotland. The book contains several attractive and interesting photographs.—*Times Literary Supplement.*

Our traveller writes lucidly and uncloggedly, and with abundant historical anecdotes, about the Highlands and the Lowlands, about birds and burns and old books, about Galloway and the Covenanters, and Cromarty and Innerpeffray and the Borderland. . . . But the reader must appreciate Dr Barnett's prevailing clean, clear prose nevertheless. His style is as refreshing as a day among the heather.—*John o' London's Weekly.*

BORDER BY-WAYS
& LOTHIAN LORE

By Rev. Dr T. RATCLIFFE BARNETT

CONTENTS

With 29 full-page illustrations from photographs by Robert M. Adam.
Crown 8vo, cloth. Pp. xii + 228. Published price 6/- net.

Press Reviews

Border By-ways and Lothian Lore links up past and present so pleasantly that it is indispensable to the rambler and a veritable source of refreshment to the stay-at-home, for Dr Barnett has not only the observant eye and an intimate knowledge of historical lore, but he has the art of conveying something of the speech and manners of the people and of the atmosphere of romance that hangs over all. . . . Dr Barnett is a genuine lover of nature, steeped in poetry and a fine appreciation of beauty, and his book clearly reveals it. The illustrations, admirably reproduced from photographs by Mr Robert M. Adam, are in keeping with the lofty standard of the subject-matter.—*Weekly Scotsman.*